Public Policy and Climate Change

Politics, Philosophy and Economics

World Scientific Lecture Notes in Economics and Policy

ISSN: 2630-4872

The World Scientific Lecture Notes in Economics and Policy series is aimed to produce lecture note texts for a wide range of economics disciplines, both theoretical and applied at the undergraduate and graduate levels. Contributors to the series are highly ranked and experienced professors of economics who see in publication of their lectures a mission to disseminate the teaching of economics in an affordable manner to students and other readers interested in enriching their knowledge of economic topics. The series was formerly titled World Scientific Lecture Notes in Economics.

Published:

Vol. 20: *Public Policy and Climate Change: Politics, Philosophy and Economics*
by John Quiggin

Vol. 19: *Lectures in Applied Environmental Economics and Policy*
by Xepapadeas Anastasios

Vol. 18: *International Economics and Policy: An Introduction to Globalization and Inequality*
by Keith E. Maskus

For the complete list of volumes in this series, please visit
www.worldscientific.com/series/wslnep

World Scientific Lecture Notes in Economics and Policy – Vol. 20

Public Policy and Climate Change

Politics, Philosophy and Economics

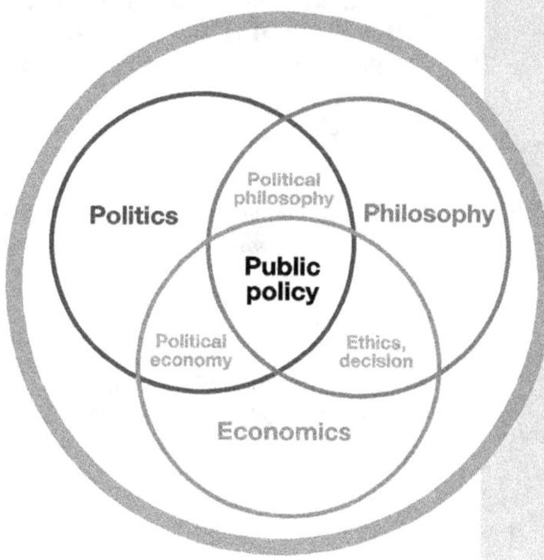

John Quiggin
University of Queensland, Australia

World Scientific

NEW JERSEY • LONDON • SINGAPORE • BEIJING • SHANGHAI • HONG KONG • TAIPEI • CHENNAI • TOKYO

Published by

World Scientific Publishing Co. Pte. Ltd.
5 Toh Tuck Link, Singapore 596224
USA office: 27 Warren Street, Suite 401-402, Hackensack, NJ 07601
UK office: 57 Shelton Street, Covent Garden, London WC2H 9HE

British Library Cataloguing-in-Publication Data
A catalogue record for this book is available from the British Library.

World Scientific Lecture Notes in Economics and Policy — Vol. 20
PUBLIC POLICY AND CLIMATE CHANGE
Politics, Philosophy and Economics

ISBN 978-981-12-9022-0 (hardcover)
ISBN 978-981-12-9061-9 (paperback)
ISBN 978-981-12-9023-7 (ebook for institutions)
ISBN 978-981-12-9024-4 (ebook for individuals)

For any available supplementary material, please visit
https://www.worldscientific.com/worldscibooks/10.1142/13760#t=suppl

Desk Editors: Aanand Jayaraman/Yulin Jiang

Typeset by Stallion Press
Email: enquiries@stallionpress.com

About the Author

John Quiggin is Professor of Economics at the University of Queensland. He is a prominent research economist and commentator on Australian and international economic policy. He has authored over 2000 publications, including 10 books and over 300 refereed journal articles, in fields such as decision theory, environmental economics, and industrial organization. He is an active contributor to Australian public debate in a wide range of traditional and social media.

Contents

Introduction

A degree in Politics, Philosophy, and Economics (PPE) was first offered by the University of Oxford in 1921. The Oxford PPE degree has produced numerous Prime Ministers of Britain as well as other countries, including Australia and Pakistan.

The PPE degree was for many years the distinctive product of Oxford. However, in recent decades, PPE programs have been offered by a large number of UK universities (Cambridge being a notable exception) and, increasingly, by universities around the world.

As in its original Oxford version, the PPE degree may be seen as an alternative to traditional classical and liberal arts degrees. It provides students with a range of approaches to critical thinking, more directly relevant to modern society than classical or literary studies, but without a narrow disciplinary or vocational focus.

The idea of critical thinking is central to discussions of the role of higher education but difficult to pin down to a definition. A standard definition, endorsed by the American Philosophical Association is as follows:

> *Purposeful, self-regulatory judgment which results in interpretation, analysis, evaluation, and inference as well as explanation of the evidential, conceptual and methodological considerations on which a judgment is based.*

This concept of critical thinking is epistemic, that is, focused on how we learn and reason, and is, on the face of it, unrelated to any particular use to which the results of critical thinking might be put. However, the prevalence of Oxford PPE degrees among the British political class suggests that this kind of critical thinking is unlikely to produce a fundamental challenge to the existing social order.

A comparison of critical thinking with a related but importantly different idea, critical pedagogy, is given by Burbules and Berk who say the following:

> *The Critical Pedagogy tradition begins from a very different starting point. It regards specific belief claims, not primarily as propositions to be assessed for their truth content, but as parts of systems of belief and action that have aggregate effects within the power structures of society. It asks first about these systems of belief and action, who benefits? The primary preoccupation of Critical Pedagogy is with social injustice and how to transform inequitable, undemocratic, or oppressive institutions and social relations.*

The PPE program at the University of Queensland is organized around the idea of 'wicked problems'. These are policy problems that are not amenable to simple technical solutions because they involve a complex interplay of policy objectives, interest groups, and theoretical perspectives.

The idea of 'wicked problems' helps to illuminate alternative views of critical thinking. The term was first used in the late 1960s, a period in which radical criticism of the existing social system was surging. It reflects a reaction against the 'technocratic' thinking of the mid-20th century, in which social problems of all kinds were seen as essentially technical and amenable to well-designed solutions. Critical thinking in the epistemic sense was needed to understand these problems and to assess alternative solutions.

By contrast, wicked problems are those "which are ill-formulated, where the information is confusing, where there are many clients and decision makers with conflicting values, and where the ramifications in the whole system are thoroughly confusing" (Churchman 1967). The element of conflict, central to the concerns of critical pedagogy, turns out to be crucial.

The course for which these lectures were prepared deals with the topic of climate policy, sometimes regarded as a 'super-wicked' problem.

The primary disciplinary framework is that of economics, but the course also draws on political and philosophical perspectives.

A central theme is the concept of opportunity cost. Economists regard opportunity cost, rather than monetary cost, as the true measure of cost. To sum up, the opportunity cost of anything of value is what you must give up to get it. This is an idea that seems simple enough when it is first presented but turns out to be unexpectedly subtle.

The lesson of opportunity cost is easy to state, but hard to learn. Only by considering a wide range of choices, and looking for the foregone opportunity involved, is it possible to acquire an intuitive grasp of the issues. The problem of global heating involves a great many of these choices.

Lecture 1

Introduction to the Course

Lecture 1 begins by setting out the central claims behind the desire to offer a PPE course.

The first claim is that the disciplines of politics, philosophy, and economics overlap in ways that make a joint study a fruitful alternative to the more common approach of specializing in one of them.

The second, stronger, claim is that the study of public policy is at the intersection of the PPE disciplines. This is illustrated by the Venn diagram.

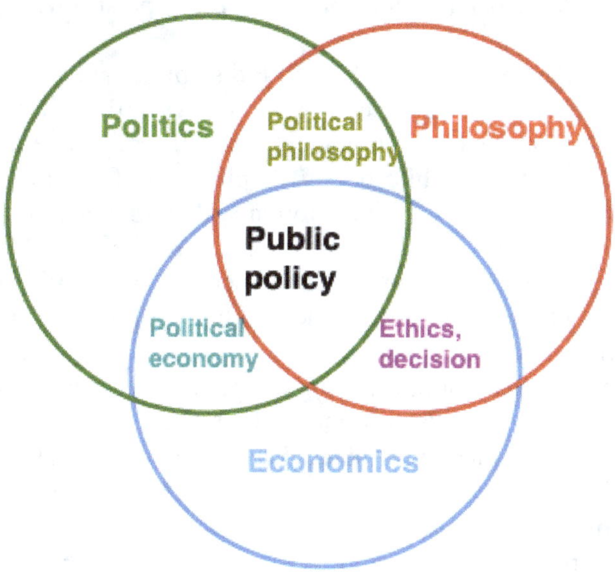

To spell out this argument, let's consider political science, philosophy, and economics in turn; the relevance of political science ought to be self-evident. The ultimate questions of what goals ought to be pursued through public policy are philosophical in nature. And, most relevantly for this book, nearly all public policy issues revolve around choices where the economic concept of opportunity cost is a crucial concern. This is true even when the debate is not discussed in monetary terms.

Even more interesting is the long-standing overlap between the disciplines of political science, philosophy, and economics. Much of economics is concerned with relatively technical issues, such as the analysis of demand and production. But, there is also a large overlap with political science, often referred to as political economy, and with philosophy, in areas such as ethics (or in economic terminology, welfare economics) and decision theory. Similarly, politics and philosophy meet in the field of political philosophy. The study of public policy requires consideration of all three disciplines and is the core of any PPE course.

These areas of overlap do not necessarily imply interdisciplinary cooperation. Researchers and policymakers from different disciplinary backgrounds have different views about what is important, different theoretical frameworks, and different criteria for what constitutes good work. For example, economists are much more concerned with mathematical rigor than political scientists or philosophers. The task of PPE is, ideally, to transcend these barriers and bring all these perspectives to bear on policy problems.

Although the perspectives of the PPE disciplines are always necessary to understand public policy, they are not always sufficient. Other factors (scientific, sociological, psychological, and cultural) have a bearing on particular decisions in public policy. Application of the PPE disciplines must be informed by perspectives from a wide range of disciplines.

The primary focus of the course is on 'global heating'. As the consequences of a hotter global climate have become more evident, this term has replaced alternatives such as the anodyne 'global warming' and the uninformative 'climate change' (as critics regularly point out, the climate is always changing). Global heating is the long-term increase in global average temperatures, caused primarily by human activity.

This lecture begins with some background information on global heating. Global temperatures have increased by nearly 1.5 °C since the beginning of large-scale use of coal, oil, and gas in the late 19th century. The effects are already being felt in the form of severe heat waves and climatic disasters. These are only going to get worse as heating accelerates.

We have been aware of the danger of global heating for 50 years, and the evidence of human-caused warming was already strong 30 years ago. Yet, efforts to respond to the problem have been patchy and inadequate.

Beginning with the 1992 'Earth Summit' in Rio de Janeiro, world leaders have made repeated attempts to agree on a path to stabilization of the global climate: at Kyoto in 1997, Copenhagen in 2010, Paris in 2015, and Glasgow in 2021, along with smaller annual meetings. Some progress has been made, but there has been a lot of backsliding.

Emissions of carbon dioxide and other greenhouse gases have continue to grow. According to some analyses, we now appear to be approaching a plateau. But, stabilizing the global climate requires substantial cuts in emissions by 2030 and decarbonization of the economy by 2050.

The inability of the world to reach an effective policy agreement reflects the fact that climate change is, in the terminology of public policy, a 'wicked problem', or even the first member of a new category of 'super-wicked problems'. Brian Head, who also teaches in the UQ PPE program, stated the following:

> *The concept of wicked problems emerged during the era of Lyndon B Johnson's 'Great Society' programs in the late 1960s, when there were polarised views about how to address major problems of inequality, unemployment and racial discrimination in the big US cities. Debates raged between the rational planners, the incremental conservatives, and the leaders of protest movements. Could federal programs solve these problems? Federal money began to flow into city administrations to fund public works projects; federal legislation attempted to secure civil and political rights; and several programs were established to improve social security and welfare.*
>
> *Amid the turmoil, city planners were developing schemes to improve the built environment and social researchers were developing proposals to improve the inter-connected issues of jobs, education, health and criminality. Academics at the University of California, Berkeley, joined in the social analysis and the policy debates. On the one hand, the public policy and management scholars, led by Wildavsky, argued that the program was poorly designed and poorly implemented because it presumed excellence in coordination and high levels of information. On the*

other hand, the urban design scholars, led by Rittel and Webber, argued that complex problems could only be advanced through dialogue and collaboration, taking account of the inherent differences in stakeholders' values and perspectives. They coined the term 'wicked problems' to designate the underlying dilemmas of working with multiple stakeholders and the impossibility of reaching a 'correct' solution.

Climate change adds additional difficulties, leading to the 'super-wicked' description: The problem must be solved urgently and nearly all actors have conflicting interests, contributing to the problem with some of their actions, while seeking to resolve it with others.

The super-wicked nature of the global heating problem is illustrated by the Australian experience. Climate policy has played a central role in every change of national leadership in Australia since 2007 (there have been six or seven), ending the careers of multiple prime ministers. Even now, we are little closer to a resolution.

In summary, we need to understand how the PPE disciplines can help resolve this intractable problem. We have our work cut out for us.

Politics, Philosophy and Economics

- **Politics**: How do societies organize and govern themselves?
  - political systems, political behavior, voting and elections
- **Philosophy**: General and fundamental questions:
  - existence and reality, knowledge and belief, ethics, logic.
- **Economics**: The allocation of resources:
  - production, consumption, markets and planning.

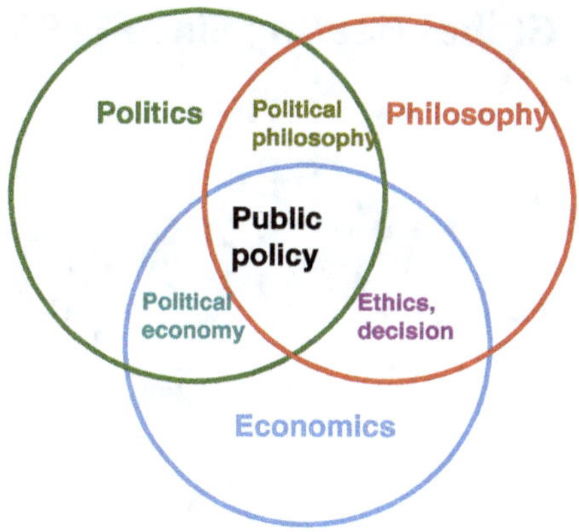

Global Heating

- Mean global temperatures have increased by nearly 1.5 °C since 1880.
- Rate of change is accelerating.
- These are caused primarily by human activity:
  - burning carbon-based fuels;
  - use of other greenhouse gases;
  - tree clearance and other land use.
- Current trends are likely to reach 3 degrees above pre-industrial by 2100.
- Effects already being felt: heatwaves, fires and floods, species extinction.
- Potential long-term consequences range from dangerous to catastrophic.

Global Heating Since 1880

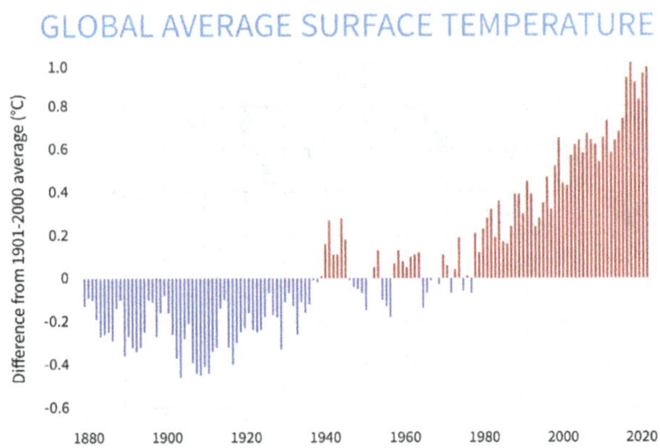

Source: NOAA, https://www.climate.gov/news-features/understanding-climate/climate-change-global-temperature.

Nearly 30 Years of Global Efforts

- The global efforts began with 'Earth Summit', Rio De Janeiro 1992.
- Kyoto Protocol 1997 and Paris Agreement 2015 are significant.
- Despite some progress, lots of backsliding can be noted.
- At different times, US and China have been leaders and laggards.
- Consistent progress could be noted only in EU:
  - Russian invasion of Ukraine has complicated this.

Where Are We Now?

- Although progress can be seen in some areas, emissions are still increasing.
- There is a need to reduce to zero by 2050 and cut substantially by 2030.
- Current policies are nowhere near adequate for this target.

Wicked Problems

- no single source of disciplinary expertise to define and understand the problem:
  - general or issue-specific distrust of experts and expertise;
- big gains and losses for large groups;
- competing cultural/social values;
- interaction between economic and cultural conflicts makes things worse.

Climate Change as a Super-Wicked Problem

- Time is running out.
- No central authority.
- Those seeking to end the problem are also causing it.

Major Source of Political Conflict in Australia

- This is central to every change of leadership at the federal level since 2007 (there have been many).
- Economic and cultural/philosophical conflicts are intertwined.
- Economic issues are poorly understood by most.

Transcending Disciplines

- Work is needed from many different disciplinary perspectives:
  - Natural science, social science, humanities.
  - These perspectives sometimes complement each other and sometimes conflict:
    - Social sciences rely on the findings of natural science and may help inform research priorities.
    - Economists and philosophers often think differently about ethics.
    - Interdisciplinary/transdisciplinary research is hard.
- This course primarily focuses on economics, but will draw on politics and philosophy.

Lecture 2

The Science of Climate Change

A particularly notable feature of the Internet era is the widespread belief that it is possible for untrained people to 'do their own research' on complex issues like global heating. Typically, this entails entering some search terms into an 'engine' such as Google and selecting those results that appeal to the preconceived 'skeptical' beliefs of the 'researcher'. This procedure works reasonably well in a search for consumer goods, the advertising for which is the main source of Google's revenue.

Unfortunately, successful use of simple research tools for shopping leads to forms of overconfidence, variously described as the 'beginner's bubble' and the Dunning–Kruger effect. Broadly speaking, the result is that the more poorly informed people are, the higher they are likely to rate their own knowledge and understanding.

Nowhere is this more true than in relation to climate science. Any discussion of the issue will attract a large number of commenters (mostly male and mostly middle aged or older), claiming to refute mainstream science. At best, these claims are based on a largely irrelevant background in fields like mining engineering. More commonly, these 'skeptics' don't understand even basic science and are relying on what they have found on the Internet.

Any serious attempt to understand the issues surrounding climate change shows that no single person can possibly understand all the issues in detail. Study of climate change involves complex issues, drawing on many different scientific disciplines such as the following:

- Chemistry (how does the greenhouse effect work?).
- Physics (how does the earth's energy budget work?).

- Climatology (how should we model and predict global climate systems?).
- Astronomy (how does the energy output of the sun vary over time?).
- Biology (how do living organisms respond to climate change?).
- Statistics (do apparent trends in temperature reflect human influence or random variations?).

At least as relevant as any of these natural science issues are the problems raised by the PPE disciplines. What are the costs and benefits of alternative courses of action? What choices are politically (in)feasible and what determines this? What are our individual and collective rights and ethical duties?

This lecture provides a comprehensive overview of the physical science behind global warming. It delves into the following critical topics:

1. **The Greenhouse Effect Origin:** Exploring the chemistry and physics behind the greenhouse effect and shedding light on its discovery by pioneering researchers, such as Eunice Foot, John Tyndall, and Svante Arrhenius.
2. **Historical Climate Change Context:** Contrasting the recent history of global warming with the much slower natural climate changes that have occurred over geological time scales.
3. **Global Warming Observation and IPCC:** Tracing the observation of global warming, which began gaining prominence in the 1970s and 1980s, leading to the establishment of the Intergovernmental Panel on Climate Change (IPCC).
4. **Current State of Knowledge:** Summarizing the current state of knowledge, emphasizing the undeniable warming trend, and recognizing that human activities are the primary driver of this phenomenon.
5. **Main Greenhouse Gases and Emission Sources:** Providing insights into the primary greenhouse gases responsible for global warming and identifying the key sources of these emissions.
6. **Parallels of Ozone Hole and Climate Action:** Discussing the ozone hole, a prior environmental challenge caused by emissions of chlorofluorocarbons (CFCs), and highlighting the successful efforts to address it in the 1990s, despite initial resistance from groups now opposing action on global warming.

7. **Climate Sensitivity:** Exploring the concept of climate sensitivity, which quantifies the equilibrium change in global temperature resulting from a doubling of atmospheric CO_2-equivalent concentration.
8. **IPCC Projections:** Outlining how the IPCC reports projections of global warming, providing valuable insights into future climate scenarios.
9. **Global Warming Outcomes:** Summarizing the main consequences of global warming, including heat waves and other extreme weather events that have become increasingly frequent and severe.

This lecture aims to provide a comprehensive understanding of the science and implications of global warming, drawing on historical insights and current research to shed light on this pressing global issue.

Summing Up

Global heating presents a pressing and undeniable challenge that demands immediate attention. The reality is indisputable, with overwhelming scientific consensus pointing to the fact that the global climate is undergoing significant and frequent alterations.

Human activity has been unequivocally identified as the primary cause of global heating. The emission of greenhouse gases, largely driven by activities such as burning fossil fuels and deforestation, has disrupted the earth's delicate balance. As a result, we are witnessing tangible changes in our environment, including rising global temperatures, more frequent and severe weather events, and shifts in ecosystems. These changes are not just distant threats but are harming communities and ecosystems around the world today.

Some changes have already become evident, and more change is inevitable. This reality underscores the critical need for concerted global efforts to mitigate and adapt to these shifts. The acceleration of heating not only guarantees further transformations but also raises the prospect of increasingly severe and widespread damage to our planet and its ecosystems. Therefore, addressing global heating is an urgent imperative.

Readings

IPCC (2023) Synthesis report of the IPCC Sixth Assessment Report (AR6).
UN Climate Change (2023) History of the Convention. https://unfccc.int/process/the-convention/history-of-the-convention.

The Science of Climate Change

- Study of climate change involves complex issues drawing on many different scientific disciplines:
  - Chemistry (How does the greenhouse effect work?);
  - Physics (How does Earth's energy budget work?);
  - Climatology (How should we model and predict global climate systems?);
  - Astronomy (How does the energy output of the sun vary over time?);
  - Biology (How do living organisms respond to climate change?);
  - Statistics (Do apparent trends in temperature reflect human influence or random variations?);
  - not to mention PPE disciplines.

A Multidisciplinary Problem

- No individual can possibly master the expertise needed to fully understand all of these issues, even with a lifetime of study.
- But, many commentators with little or no relevant education imagine they can do so in their spare time.
- We will have a quick overview.

The Greenhouse Effect

- A misnomer: Greenhouses don't (primarily) work this way.
- Greenhouse gases absorb and emit radiant energy.
- The atmosphere allows the sun's rays to pass through, but traps heat sun that would otherwise be radiated, maintaining a higher surface temperature consistent with (current forms of) life out to space.
- Mars: No atmosphere, very low surface temperature.
- Venus: Runaway greenhouse effect, surface temperature hot enough to melt lead.
- Earth: In the "Goldilocks zone", at least for now.

Discovery of the Greenhouse Effect

- This effect was first discovered experimentally by Eunice Foote (1856):
  - As a woman, she was not allowed to present her own paper.
  - John Tyndall (1859) published the same idea and got primary credit.
- The first quantitative predictions were made by Arrhenius (1896):
  - He first estimated climate sensitivity at 5.5 C and then lowered it to 2.1.
  - This was very close to the modern range.
  - He was Swedish and thought a warmer climate would be good.

Global Heating (and Cooling) Over Time

- Climate has changed greatly over time:
  - Ice ages: We are currently in an interglacial period of Quaternary Ice Age, which started 10,000 years ago.
  - Continental drift was proposed.
  - But, on geological timescales, it would be tens of thousands to millions of years:
    - much smaller, and more localised, variations on 1,000-year timescales;
    - "Little Ice Age" in Northern Europe.
- Increase in temperatures have been noted since the late 19th century:
  - This was caused by human activity.
  - Relative stability in mid-C20: Greenhouse heating offset by particulate pollution.
  - Heating since 1970, overlaid on natural cycles such as El Nino/ Southern Oscillation.

The Discovery of Global Heating

- https://history.aip.org/climate/summary.htm.
- Keeling showed an increase in atmospheric CO_2 (1960).
- Evidence of heating was found by the 1970s, partly offset by dust and smog.
- See US National Academy of Sciences (1979).
- 1988 was the hottest year in global record:
  - James Hansen predicted likely heating with three emissions scenarios.
  - Scenario B prediction was very accurate so far.

IPCC

- IPCC stands for the Intergovernmental Panel on Climate Change.
- This is the UN body established in 1988 to summarize research on the science of climate change, impacts and adaption.
- IPCC has released a series of assessment reports, the most recent one being the Sixth Assessment Report (2023).

Current State of Knowledge

- Climate has warmed by nearly 1.5 degrees since 1880:
  - beginning of instrumental record;
  - before significant human effects on global climate.
- Human actions are primarily responsible for this.
- Current trajectory suggests likely warming of 3 degrees.
- Severe costs are likely if warming exceeds 2 degrees.
- It is desirable to keep warming to 1.5 degrees:
  - We are certain to overshoot this.
  - We need enough decarbonization to cool climate after 2050.

Global Heating Since 1880

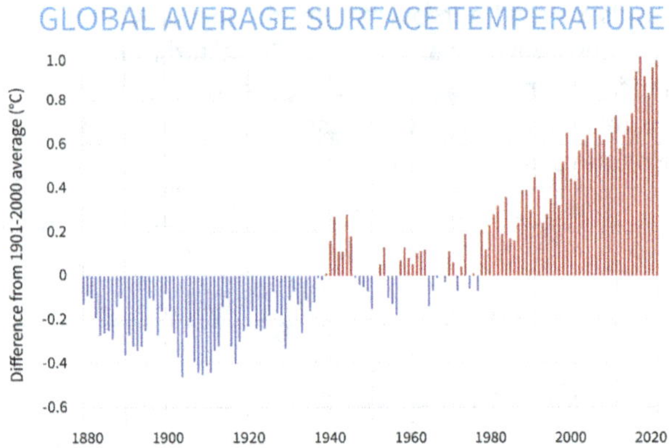

Source: NOAA, https://www.climate.gov/news-features/understanding-climate/climate-change-global-temperature.

Greenhouse Gases

- Carbon dioxide (CO_2);
- Methane (CH_4);
- Nitrous oxide (N_2O);
- Chlorofluorocarbons (CFCs);
- Hydrofluorocarbons (includes HCFCs and HFCs);
- Water vapor (H_2O).

The Main Greenhouse Gases

- **Carbon dioxide (CO_2):** Natural carbon cycle; pre-industrial concentration of about 270–290 ppm; increase generated by burning carbon-based "fossil fuels" (oil, coal, natural gas), and by land clearing.
- **Methane (CH_4):** Increase generated by ruminant (cows and sheep) belches and rice paddy cultivation, leaks from natural gas wells and pipelines (natural gas is methane).
- **Nitrous oxide (NO_2):** Increase generated by use of nitrogen fertilizers.
- **CFCs & HCFC:** All human-created; used as propellants and refrigerants; now being phased out.
- **Water vapor:** Crucial source of feedback; not directly affected by human activity.
- **Key point:** Just about everything humans do has some effect on emissions, positive or negative:
  - Human activity now dominates the planet.
  - Stabilizing the global climate has implications for all sectors of the economy and society.

CO_2 Equivalents and Atmospheric Concentrations

- Each of the main greenhouse gases may be described in terms of a CO_2-equivalent. This relates the global warming potential of 1 ppm of the gas in question to that of 1 ppm of CO_2.
- Measures of atmospheric concentration of greenhouses gases are obtained by converting and adding these together.
- Global warming potential depends on residence time and radiative forcing
- Residence time: How long does gas stay in the atmosphere?

Carbon Dioxide (CO_2)

- Natural carbon cycle accounts for most CO_2.
- Anthropogenic emissions arise from the combustion of carbon C+2O -> CO_2.
- This accounts for around 65 percent of warming.
- Burning of carbon-based fuels, coal, oil, and natural gas
  - electricity generation;
  - heating;
  - industrial uses: steel, cement.
- Excess emissions remain in the atmosphere for 20–200 years, some potentially for thousands of years.

Methane (CH_4)

- This is a more powerful greenhouse gas than CO_2 but with shorter residence time.
- This accounts for around 20 percent of warming.
- As natural gas, this is burned to produce CO_2 and H_2O (water vapor), with less warming potential per unit of energy than carbon fuels (coal and oil).
- Primary sources included paddy rice, belches from ruminants (cattle and sheep), and leakage from gas production, particularly fracking.
- Possible catastrophic feedback of natural methane can be released by warming.

Nitrous oxide (NO_2)

- This is a powerful greenhouse gas, 300 times more so than CO_2.
- NO_2 has a long residence time (100 years).
- NO_2 accounts for about 6 percent of warming.
- Primary source includes the use of nitrogen fertilizers.

CFC, HCFC, HFC

- CFC refers to chlorofluorocarbons; HCFC refers to hydrochlorofluorocarbons.
  - These are used as propellants and refrigerants.
  - These caused a hole in the ozone layer.
  - These were phased out under the Montreal Protocol (1987).
  - Hydrofluorocarbon (HFC) replacement doesn't deplete the ozone layer.
  - All are potent greenhouse gases.

Particles and Aerosols

- Small particles suspended in the atmosphere are called aerosols. They include soot, dust ash, and sulfates. At the ground level, particulates are an important and dangerous form of air pollution.
- However, some particulates reflect incoming sunlight and thereby offset the impact of greenhouse gases.
- Problem: As we reduce air pollution at the ground level, we may exacerbate global warming.
- Some advocates of "geoengineering" have suggested the deliberate use of aerosols to increase the albedo (reflectivity) of the atmosphere.
- https://earthobservatory.nasa.gov/features/Aerosols.

Atmospheric Concentrations

- These were first systematically measured at Mauna Loa, Hawaii.
- Keeling curve was observed.
- There was a steady upward trend, but calculation shows that only about half of CO_2 emitted ends up in the atmosphere: the "airborne fraction".
- Some are captured by the carbon cycle, but most end up in the ocean. This is not harmless! CO_2 makes water more acid, thereby making it harder for coral reefs to form (acid dissolves limestone). Reef ecosystems are already among the most vulnerable to warming and may also be affected by increasingly severe cyclones — a triple whammy.

The Keeling Curve

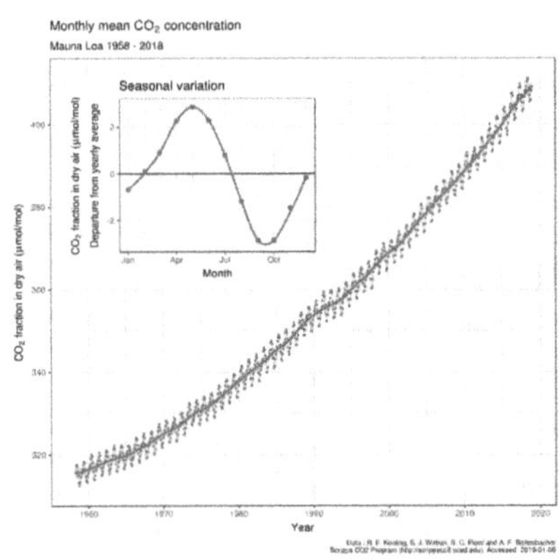

Source: https://en.wikipedia.org/wiki/Keeling_Curve.

Climate Sensitivity

- The equilibrium change in global temperature would arise from a doubling of atmospheric CO_2 equivalent concentrations:
  - Since pre-industrial concentration was 270–290 ppm, doubling would mean stabilization around 550 ppm.
- IPCC AR6 (2021) sensitivity range 2.5–4 °C (likely):
  - The central estimate of 3 °C changed since NAS (1979) (or much since 1900), but the range tightened in AR6 "confidence" has increased greatly.
  - Equilibrium has not been reached immediately; Transient Climate Response is estimated at 1–2.5 °C.

IPCC Measure of Confidence

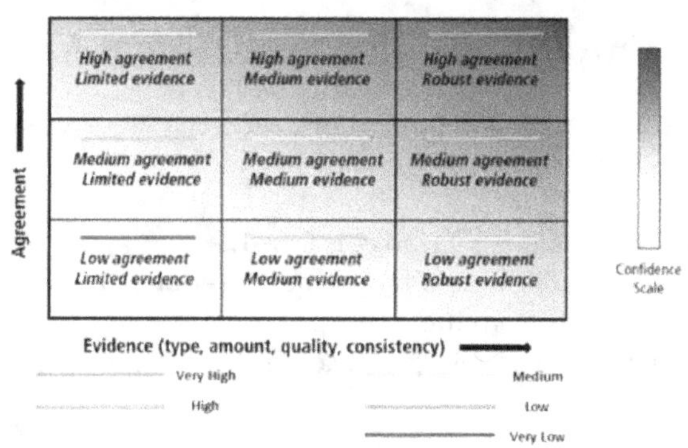

Figure 1: Confidence levels are a combination of level of agreement and evidence. There are five levels, shown with colours. (IPCC 2013)

Source: https://theconversation.com/lost-in-translation-confidence-and-certainty-in-climate-science-17181.

IPCC Likelihood

Table 1. Likelihood Scale	
Term*	**Likelihood of the Outcome**
Virtually certain	99-100% probability
Very likely	90-100% probability
Likely	66-100% probability
About as likely as not	33 to 66% probability
Unlikely	0-33% probability
Very unlikely	0-10% probability
Exceptionally unlikely	0-1% probability

Implications for Global Heating

- If CO_2 is stabilized at 550 ppm, there will be an equilibrium warming of 1.5–4.5.
- For 450 ppm, median is 2, range is 1–3.
- For 350 ppm, median is 1, range is 0.5–1.5.
- We are already at 400, so a target of 350 requires the removal of greenhouse gases from the atmosphere.
- Plausible pathways to 450 may also imply "overshoot".

Outcomes of Global Heating

- Higher average temperatures (obviously 1):
  - more on land than on sea;
  - more at night than daytime.
- Higher maximums and minimums:
  - more heat waves, less cold snaps.
- Dry areas get drier, wet areas get wetter:
  - more extreme events (severe cyclones, floods).
- These effects are already evident:
  - "attribution problem" largely resolved: https://www.ametsoc.org/ams/index.cfm/publications/bulletin-of-the-american-meteorological-society-bams/explaining-extreme-events-from-a-climate-perspective/;
  - scientists have identified extreme weather events that they said could not have happened without warming of the climate through human-induced climate change.

Effects of Global Heating

- agriculture;
- sea level;
- health;
- environmental.

The Burning Embers Diagram

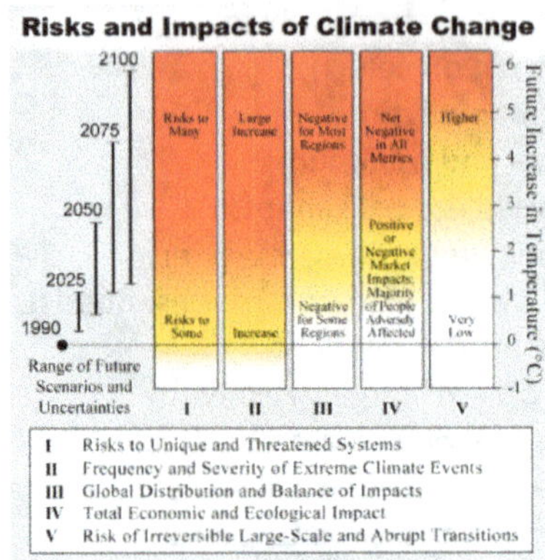

Source: IPCC TAR.

Environmental Effects of Climate Change

- Species extinction
- Ecosystems 'migrate' toward the poles:
  - But this happens too slowly to keep up with climate change;
  - 'Island' ecosystems cannot shift.
- Coral reefs — A triple whammy:
  - warming and bleaching;
  - acidification due to CO_2;
  - more intense cyclones.

Agriculture

- Modest warming is beneficial in cold climates, but harmful in hot climates.
- Rapid warming is harmful generally.
- CO_2 fertilization is important.
- Note drought impacts in SE Australia and similar climates.

Sea Level

- Modest and gradual expansions can happen due to heating.
- Melting ice caps are more rapid than expected.
- Cyclones and storm surges: Fewer are possible but these will be more intense.
- This is costly because so much infrastructure is located at the seafront
- This is already evident.

Health

- Heat waves cause many deaths.
- Reduced cold severity is only a partial offset.
- There is a greater range of tropical diseases.

Thinking about Costs

- Rapid change is usually bad:
  - Infrastructure and institutions are based on the current climate.
  - Adjustment is costly.
  - This is particularly so for ecosystems: moving toward the poles, but too slowly.
- Costs and benefits are mixed for modest warming, costs predominate for warming over 2 degrees.
- A convex damage function can be used.

Summing Up

- Climate change is a real and urgent problem.
- Human activity is the primary cause.
- Some changes have already happened and more is inevitable.
- More and faster climate change means more and more severe damage.

Lecture 3

From Rio to Glasgow

No matter where carbon-based fuels are produced and no matter where they are burned to emit greenhouse gases, they are rapidly mixed in the atmosphere and their effects are felt throughout the world. Moreover, while people and nations differ radically in the emissions they generate, everyone uses energy and nearly everyone contributes to global heating to some extent.

In these circumstances, some form of international cooperation is essential if the problem is to be solved, or at least mitigated. This fact was recognized almost as soon as global heating was recognized as a potential problem. The United Nations Environment Programme established the Intergovernmental Panel on Climate Change (IPCC) in 1988. Four years later, at the Rio de Janeiro 'Earth Summit', 154 states signed the United Nations Framework Convention on Climate Change (UNFCCC).

Conferences of the Parties to the Convention have been held annually since then, with varying degrees of success. But, more than 30 years after the Earth Summit, the problem of climate change remains a wicked one, with contention over just about every aspect of the policy response.

This lecture deals with the history of international negotiations over global heating and the prospects for future agreement.

Before considering global heating, we will look at a closely related problem that was addressed successfully: the 'ozone hole' created by emissions of chlorofluorocarbons (CFCs), used by refrigerants and propellants for spray cans. The chemical reactions by which small quantities of CFCs could destroy large amounts of ozone were discovered in the 1970s and led to the award of the Nobel Prize in 1995. But, it was not until the observation of declining ozone levels over the South Pole (the ozone hole) that any serious action was taken.

Despite some resistance from industry, and the emergence of a group of professional 'skeptics', there was rapid international agreement on the Vienna Convention for the Protection of the Ozone Layer (1985) and the associated Montreal Protocol (1987). Developed countries took the lead in phasing out the use of CFCs, while less developed countries received aid and technical assistance to follow suit over time.

By the late 1990s, the declining trend in ozone levels stabilized and slowly began to reverse. On current indications, the ozone layer should return to normal in the second half of this century.

The successful resolution of the CFC problem seemed to provide a template for action on greenhouse gases. The UN Framework Convention on Climate Change (UNFCCC) adopted at the Earth Summit, Rio de Janeiro 1992, and the Kyoto Protocol 1997 followed the same model.

Unfortunately, the success of the Montreal Protocol was not replicated. Whereas all major countries ratified the Montreal Protocol, the US, then the biggest emitter, did not ratify the Kyoto Protocol, Australia refused to ratify it until 2008, and Canada ratified it but withdrew in 2012.

The Kyoto Protocol was partially successfully, in that most developed countries met their targets. But, emissions continued to rise in US and in less developed countries. China became the world's biggest emitter, and India also grew rapidly. More importantly, Kyoto did not form the basis of a sustained move toward an international agreement or a system of international trading in emission permits.

What went wrong? This lecture explores a range of problems. The Montreal solution didn't 'scale up' to the massively larger problem of decarbonizing the economy. Industrial emitters fought harder and gave more support to scientific 'skeptics', many of whom were recruited from previous fights over CFCs and tobacco. Most significantly, climate policy became enmeshed in the culture wars that now plague every aspect of life in the US and other countries. It became a matter of personal identity for political conservatives to reject the science of climate change

Coordinated action was not achieved until the Paris Agreement of 2015, which relied on voluntary commitments rather than a legally binding treaty. Thanks largely to technological progress in carbon-free technologies, such as solar PV and wind turbines, many countries have achieved significant reductions in emissions at relatively low cost.

One important result of technological progress has been an increase in ambition. Previous agreements implied heating of 2 to 3 °C. The Paris Agreement, by contrast, sought to

> *Keep the increase in global average temperature to well below 2 °C above pre-industrial levels; and to pursue efforts to limit the increase to 1.5 °C, recognizing that this would substantially reduce the risks and impacts of climate change.*

In the remainder of this course, we will consider how the PPE disciplines can be brought to bear on the achievement of this goal.

Readings

Klekociuk, A. & Kremmul, P. (2017) After 30 years of the Montreal Protocol, the ozone layer is gradually healing. https://theconversation.com/after-30-years-of-the-montreal-protocol-the-ozone-layer-is-gradually-healing-84051.

Rae, I., (2012) Saving the ozone layer: why the Montreal Protocol worked. https://theconversation.com/saving-the-ozone-layer-why-the-montreal-protocol-worked-9249.

From Rio to Glasgow

- International climate agreements were adopted from Rio to Glasgow via Kyoto and Paris.
- Civil society pushed for decarbonization.
- The role of technology is crucial.
- The obstacles to the agreement include international political economy, interest groups, and identity politics.

The Ozone Hole: A Dress Rehearsal?

- Chlorofluorocarbons (CFCs):
  - Refrigerants and propellants are used for aerosol spray cans.
- Ozone (O_3) is a form of oxygen toxic to breathe but important to our survival:
  - Ozone layer in the atmosphere protects us from ultraviolet light.
- CFCs and some other gases react strongly with ozone:
  - Molina and Rowland (1974) (following earlier work by Crutzen on nitrous oxide);
  - Nobel Prize 1995.
- Ozone "hole" over Antarctic was discovered in 1985.
- Same processes contribute to global warming.

Rapid International Response: The Montreal Protocol

- Vienna Convention for the Protection of the Ozone Layer 1985:
  - a "framework agreement";
- Montreal Protocol (to Vienna Convention) 1987:
  - agreement on policy responses;
- Rapid phase-out of CFCs in developed countries:
  - replaced by other gases (some also greenhouse gases);
- Less developed countries given more time and technical assistance.

A Huge Success

- This has been ratified by all UN member states.
- Near-universal implementation of commitments was achieved.
- Production of CFCs was phased out by 1994:
  - Unsatisfactory replacement (HCFC) had to be phased out by 2020.
  - Alternative HFC doesn't deplete the ozone layer or contribute to climate change.
- Though the size of the ozone hole stabilized by 2007, this is now on a declining trend.

Some Warning Signs

- Initial resistance from industry:
  - DuPont, the main producer, took out full-page ads in 1975 denouncing Molina and Rowlands.
- Emergence of organized science denial:
  - Notable figures included William Happer (later appointed to NSC by Trump).
  - Most moved on to climate science denial (Baliunas, Singer, Bast, Seitz).
- Partisan division in the US:
  - GHW Bush Administration (1991–1995) was generally supportive.
  - But some Republicans supported CFC denial.

Applying the Ozone Model to Global Heating

- development of science;
- international conference under UN auspices;
- agreement to address the problem led by developed countries;
- assistance to poorer countries.

Adapting the Montreal Model

- UN Framework Convention on Climate Change (UNFCCC) was adopted at the Earth Summit, Rio de Janeiro 1992.
- Kyoto Protocol 1997 was adopted at the third Conference of the Parties to the UNFCCC (COP 3), Kyoto 1997.
- Annual Conferences of the Parties were conducted, notably including Copenhagen (2009) and Paris (2015).

Intergovernmental Panel on Climate Change (IPCC)

- This UN body was established in 1988 to summarize research on the science of climate change, impacts and adaption.
- There have been five assessment reports so far, and the next is due in 2022.
- Special Report on Global Warming of 1.5 °C was published in 2018.

Rio Earth Summit 1992

- United Nations Conference on Environment and Development was held in Rio de Janeiro on 3–14 June.
- UN Framework Convention on Climate Change (UNFCCC) was established based on First Assessment Report of IPCC.

The Kyoto Protocol, 1997

- The protocol established legal obligations for developed countries to reduce greenhouse gas emissions.
- Voluntary efforts were made by less developed (Annex II) countries.
- Targets involved modest reductions in emissions relative to baseline (usually 1990).
- US did not ratify, Australia refused to ratify until 2008, Canada ratified but withdrew in 2012. All were under centre-right or rightwing governments.
- This was effectively superseded by Paris Agreement 2015.

Outcomes

- Most developed countries met their targets.
- But emissions continued to rise in the US and in less developed countries. China became the world's biggest emitter, and India also grew rapidly.
- These did not form the basis of a sustained move to an international agreement.
- International trading in emissions permits did not develop.

What Went Wrong?

- A much bigger problem was that the Montreal solution didn't "scale up".
- Industry fought harder and gave more support to denialists:
  - could recruit them from previous fights over CFCs and tobacco;
  - Exxon funding of think tanks.
- Rise of identity politics/culture wars was obvious:
  - evident in the current division within the Australian government over coal.
- International politics played a role:
  - not as important as domestic disputes.

Merchants of Doubt

- *Merchants of Doubt* is a 2010 book by Naomi Oreskes and Erik Conway.
- The book shows how the tobacco industry developed fear, uncertainty and doubt (FUD) tactics to fight the regulation of passive smoking.
- US Tobacco industry was defeated in Master Settlement 1998:
  - Huge troves of documents were released.
- Climate denial groups adopted the FUD tactics, tobacco "experts", and thietanes:
  - Lindzen, Milloy, Singer, Seitz;
  - CEI, AEI, Cato, Heartland in US, IPA in Australia.

Identity Politics

- Attitudes to climate change are deeply bound up with personal identity for many people.
- Some environmentalists see climate change as necessitating a radical shift from a consumer society they dislike.
- Some conservatives identify themselves by opposition to "enviros".
- These attitudes have become more entrenched over time.
- Is there room for evidence-based policy in a 'post-truth' world?

What Went Right?

- Many low-cost or negative-cost ("no regrets") options were identified and implemented:
  - energy waste and inefficiency.
- Political consensus on climate action was established in most European countries.
- Renewable energy subsidies spurred research and development:
  - notably in Germany;
  - major reductions in the cost of solar PV, wind.

Copenhagen (2010)

- This was limited and unsatisfactory.
- The Chinese government aggressively resisted any legally binding agreement.
- US President Obama patched up a face-saving compromise.
- Failure contributed to the defeat of the emissions trading scheme in Australia.

Paris (2015): Restarting the Process

- Scientific evidence was close to certain:
  - This was confirmed by everyday experience.
  - This hadn't affected science deniers.
- Main players (US, EU, China, India) keen to achieve an agreement:
  - Reluctant parties (Australia, Saudi Arabia) have little room to move.
- Tech progress in renewables reduces the cost of stabilization.

Paris Agreement

- This was set up within UNFCCC, replacing Kyoto:
  - This included voluntary and national commitments in place of legally binding targets.
  - But these were more ambitious in most cases.
- Key concept included Nationally Determined Contributions (NDCs).
- Initial NDCs were clearly inadequate and had to be ramped up over time.

Goal of Climate Stabilization

- Keep the increase in global average temperature to well below 2 °C above pre-industrial levels, and pursue efforts to limit the increase to 1.5 °C, recognizing that this would substantially reduce the risks and impacts of climate change.
- This should be done by reducing emissions as soon as possible in order to "achieve a balance between anthropogenic emissions by sources and removals by sinks of greenhouse gases" in the second half of the 21st century.

Nationally Determined Commitments (NDCs)

- Each signatory made an initial unilateral commitment:
  - US emissions were 26–28 percent below 2005 levels by 2025.
  - China will have to reduce carbon intensity (emissions per unit of GDP) 60–65 percent on 2005 levels by 2030.
  - Australia will have to reduce 26–28 percent below 2005 levels by 2030.
- It would be insufficient to achieve the 450-ppm goal.
- If unchanged, imply 3 degrees of warming.

5-Yearly Stocktakes

- The idea is to ratchet up ambition.
- Initial Paris NDCs were more ambitious than implied by the Kyoto process.
- Some further progress was made in Glasgow.
- Next major stocktake would be Madrid 2025.

International Politics

- Theory suggests a free rider problem in which each country seeks to minimize its own costs while encouraging others to do more:
  - This can be seen to some extent.
  - Most countries pick a baseline and metric to make them look good.
  - But this is relatively unimportant.
- In practice, alliances cross national boundaries:
  - Environment movement operates on a global scale.
  - The same is true of climate science denial.
  - Global multinational companies are on both sides.
  - In contemporary politics, global cultural alignments Trump (!) national interest.

Scope for Voluntary International Agreement

- A few big players (US, EU, China, Russia, India) can decide most things if they agree:
  - In the absence of active resistance, four out of five are usually enough.
  - Repeated and unpredictable interactions can happen.
- Small countries then have little choice but to join the agreement.
- Governments of medium-sized countries like Australia want to "punch above their weight".
- A leading role in reaching an agreement yields prestige for the governments concerned:
  - Maybe it is worth contributing more than the necessary minimum.

Is a Ratchet Feasible?

- Past experience shows that the cost of meeting commitments has been much lower than expected.
- "Decoupling" of emissions and growth in the developed world is crucial:
  - This is partly, but only partly, explained by the 'offshoring' of manufacturing.
  - Should targets be based on the location of emissions or final consumption?
- Either way, this needs steady increases.

Other Elements

- Green Climate Fund (pledges of $10 billion);
- Loss and Damage:
  - issues of compensation and liability unresolved;
- Enhanced transparency framework:
  - a substitute for legal obligations.

Trump Administration

- Trump won the US Presidential election in 2016.
- He announced his intention to withdraw from the Paris Agreement in June 2017.
- The withdrawal took effect, on 4 November 2020, just before Trump's election defeat.
- Despite this and a range of Trump policies, coal mining and coal-fired power declined sharply.

Biden Administration

- Following steps were taken post the Inauguration on 19 January:
  - There was renewed focus on Climate Ambition Summit.
  - Biden signed the Executive order to rejoin the Paris Agreement within hours of inauguration.
  - The administration made climate a top priority.
  - Biden took steps to restrict oil and gas exploration, drilling, and pipelines.
  - The climate plan included transition policies to manage the decline of coal mining.

Earth Day Summit, 22 April 2021

- This was announced as part of US President Biden's Climate Action Plan on 28 January 2021:
  - Earth Day celebrated since 1970;
  - also date of the Paris Agreement in 2015;
  - importance of political symbolism?
- There was pressure to commit to 2050 zero target and stronger 2030 targets.
- Biden is also pushing China to move from 2060 to 2050 target date.
- Australia, Brazil and Saudi Arabia are the most notable holdout.

Glasgow COP November 2021

- What is needed?
  - A 50 percent reduction in emissions relative to 2005 (or similar) levels by 2030 is required.
- What happened?
  - Most countries, but not Australia, submitted new or revised commitments with more ambitious reductions.
- Methane is included in discussions for the first time.
- Median estimate of warming by 0.1–0.2 °C has been reduced to around 2.4 °C.
- Though there has been progress, we still have a long way to go.

The Green New Deal

- The proposal for this deal came from the progressive Democrats.
- The deal calls for rapid decarbonization of the US economy by 2030.
- This is combined with egalitarian economic policies such as a higher minimum wage.
- This is an aspiration rather than a fully specified program.
- This deal mostly failed to get through the US Congress.

Lecture 4

Opportunity Cost

Lecture 4 introduces one of the crucial ideas of the course, the concept of 'opportunity cost', and shows how it is related to the problem of the carbon budget.

We consider both private and social opportunity costs:

> *The private opportunity cost of anything is what you must give up to get it.*
>
> *The social opportunity cost of anything of value is what you and others must give up so that you can have it.*

Opportunity cost and not accounting costs or market prices is the central concept of cost for economists. The concept applies to all the choices we make as individuals and as a society. Ideally, market prices should coincide with social opportunity costs, but there are many reasons why they may not.

In my previous book *Economics in Two Lessons*, I argued that the central issues in economics could be boiled down to the following:

- **Lesson 1:** Market prices reflect and determine opportunity costs faced by consumers and producers.
- **Lesson 2:** Market prices don't reflect all the opportunity costs we face as a society.

The simplest case is that of an individual consumer, with a fixed budget, trying to decide what to consume. If the budget has been fully allocated, consuming more of any one time means consuming less of another. In a market setting, the trade-off between the two is determined by relative prices. Conversely, the decisions of consumers and producers, in aggregate, determine what those relative prices will be.

But the idea of opportunity cost applies more broadly to encompass choices:

- between allocating goods to one person or another;
- between different locations;
- between present and future.

In particular, the concept of opportunity cost is crucial in understanding the idea of the carbon budget. If the world is to have a reasonable chance of holding global warming to 2 degrees or less, the concentration of carbon dioxide and other greenhouse gasses in the atmosphere must be held below 450 ppm and ideally even less. This requirement in turn limits the total amount of carbon dioxide we can emit in the future or, in other words, the carbon budget available to us.

In this chapter, we show how the analysis of opportunity cost subject to a budget constraint applies to the case of carbon dioxide emissions. Given a global or national carbon budget, the total quantity of emissions is fixed. So, a tonne of emissions generated for one purpose is a tonne of emissions that must be reduced elsewhere if the budget constraint is to be met Opportunity cost is always relevant.

We also examine the acronym TANSTAAFL (There Ain't No Such Thing As A Free Lunch) popularized by science fiction writer Robert Heinlein and economist Milton Friedman. The original free lunches were provided by saloons in the US. Since the price of the lunch was bundled into the price of the beer that went with it, the free lunches weren't really free.

The broader point is that everything we produce and consume has an opportunity cost. If (to take a current example in Australia) the government builds a new stadium to host major sporting events, 'creating jobs' for construction workers and materials suppliers, the opportunity cost is the housing those workers and materials could otherwise have built.

Despite this, There Is Such A Thing As A Free Lunch (TISATAAFL). Technological improvements allow us to produce more with the same inputs, and the extra production is a free lunch. When new opportunities for trade are exploited, the gains from trade represent a free trade for both parties. In fact, an ideal market equilibrium can be defined exactly by the fact that there are no free lunches left on the table.

Finally, we consider some of the changes that need to be made if we are to remain within a sustainable carbon budget. The first, relatively easy step is to decarbonize the electricity supply, replacing coal and gas with wind, solar PV, and other clean technologies such as hydropower and geothermal. The expansion of nuclear power is another potential source of low-carbon energy, but in practice, it appears that the technology is too expensive to be a viable option.

With enough clean electricity, most carbon dioxide emissions can be addressed. Transport and home heating can be electrified, hydrogen can replace metallurgical coal, and so on. Less tractable sources of emissions are mostly associated with land use, including deforestation and methane emissions from rice paddies and livestock.

But there is nearly always an alternative. If we are to save the planet from climate catastrophe, we will have to give up some things we do at present and replace them with alternatives that may initially be more costly. This is the lesson of opportunity cost.

Bibliography

Meinshausen, M. *et al.* (2009) Greenhouse-gas emission targets for limiting global warming to 2°C. *Nature*, **458**, 1158, http://ecolo.org/documents/documents_in_english/CO2-Nature-09.pdf.

Quiggin, J. (2013) Is it too late to stabilise the global climate. *Australian Journal of Agricultural and Resource Economics*, **57**, 1–14, http://doi.wiley.com/10.1111/j.1467-8489.2012.00617.x.

Quiggin, J. (2019) *Economics in Two Lessons: Why Markets Work So Well, and Why They can Fail So Badly* (Chapters 1 and 2). Princeton, NJ: Princeton University Press.

What Is Opportunity Cost?

- *The opportunity cost of anything is what you must give up to get it.*
- *The SOCIAL opportunity cost of anything of value is what you AND OTHERS must give up so that you can have it.*
- For a marketed good,
  - consumers' opportunity cost is their best alternative consumption option,
  - producers' opportunity cost is the best alternative output, and
  - there must be trade-offs at the margin.
- Social opportunity cost takes account of all foregone opportunities.

Opportunity Cost Applies to All Choices

The opportunity cost applies to all the following choices:

- between different goods,
- between allocating goods to one person or another,
- between present and future,
- between different locations.

Economics in Two Lessons

- **Lesson 1**: Market prices reflect and determine opportunity costs faced by consumers and producers.
- **Lesson 2**: Market prices don't reflect all the opportunity costs we face as a society.

Economics in Two Lessons

Source: Princeton University Press, 2019.

Consumers and the Budget Constraint

- Budget is total amount available to spend.
- Relative prices determine opportunity costs.
- Preferences and prices determine choices.
- Optimization requires that relative prices equal marginal rates of substitution (MRS).

Opportunity Cost for Consumers

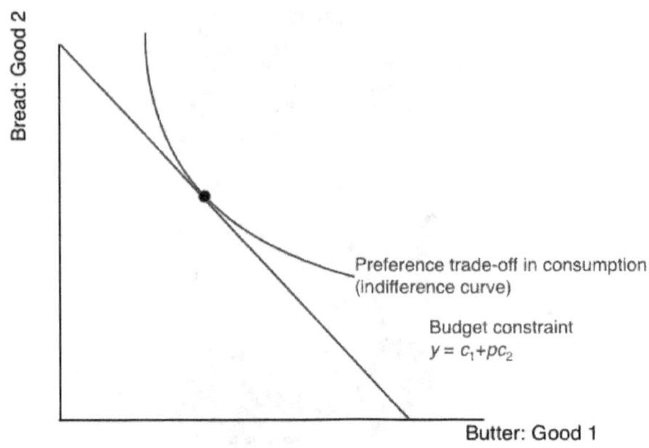

Producers and Production Possibilities

- With given resources, what can be produced?
- Production technology determines opportunity costs.
- Prices and profit maximization determine choices.
- Profit maximization requires relative prices equal marginal rate of transformation (MRT).

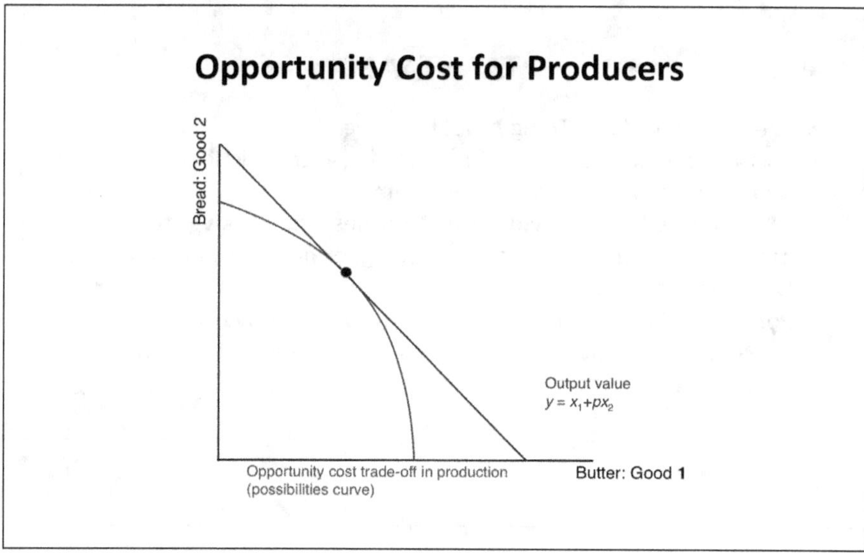
Opportunity Cost for Producers
Bread: Good 2
Output value
$y = x_1 + px_2$
Opportunity cost trade-off in production
(possibilities curve)
Butter: Good 1

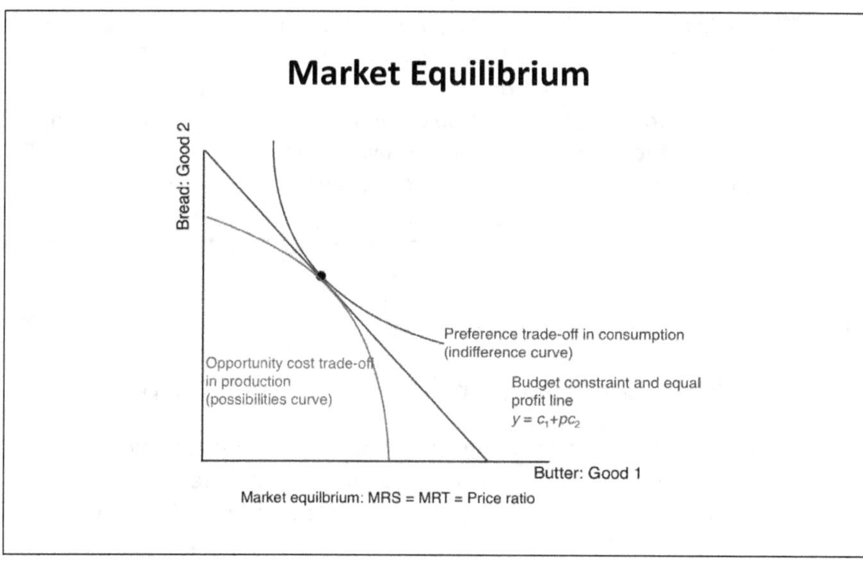
Market Equilibrium
Bread: Good 2
Preference trade-off in consumption
(indifference curve)
Opportunity cost trade-off
in production
(possibilities curve)
Budget constraint and equal
profit line
$y = c_1 + pc_2$
Butter: Good 1
Market equilibrium: MRS = MRT = Price ratio

TANSTAAFL

- There Ain't No Such Thing As A Free Lunch.
- This was popularized by Robert Heinlein (science fiction writer) and Milton Friedman (free market economist).
- US Saloons used to provide "free" lunches. The idea was that patrons would drink enough beer at higher prices to pay for lunch. Now, they offer free salted peanuts instead.
- Point is applied to "free" public services paid for by taxation.
- This relies implicitly on assumptions about competitive market equilibrium.

Free Lunches

- **TISATAAFL:** There Is Such A Thing As A Free Lunch.
- Whenever two people make an exchange that leaves them both better off, there is a free lunch.
- The opportunity cost is the value of what each party gives up, which is less than the value (to them) of what they receive.
- Technological progress is a free lunch for everyone.

Free Lunches and Market Equilibrium

- When all goods are traded and everyone has the best (for them) consumption bundle they can get at competitively determined prices, there are no remaining exchanges that would make both parties better off.
- No free lunches left on the table, or more formally, Pareto-optimal theorem.
- This is the (first) Fundamental Theorem of Welfare Economics.
- The second theorem is that any Pareto-optimal outcome can be supported as a competitive equilibrium.

What About Climate?

- Assume we have a carbon price (can-opener joke).
- Assume also that society can express its preference for a stable climate (measured in tonnes of CO_2 emissions avoided).
- Then we can draw the same diagram.

The Carbon Budget

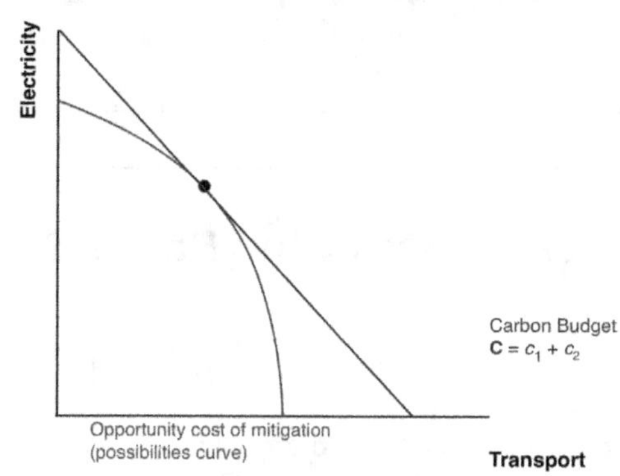

Interpretation: all emissions are equal, $p = 1$

The Carbon Price Equilibrium

- Carbon price is equal to marginal damage caused by an additional tonne of CO_2: climate vs consumption indifference curve (blue).
- Carbon price is also equal to the marginal cost of mitigation: possibilities curve (red).
- In a perfect competitive market, with carbon prices, these two would be equal.

Ideal Carbon Price Equilibrium

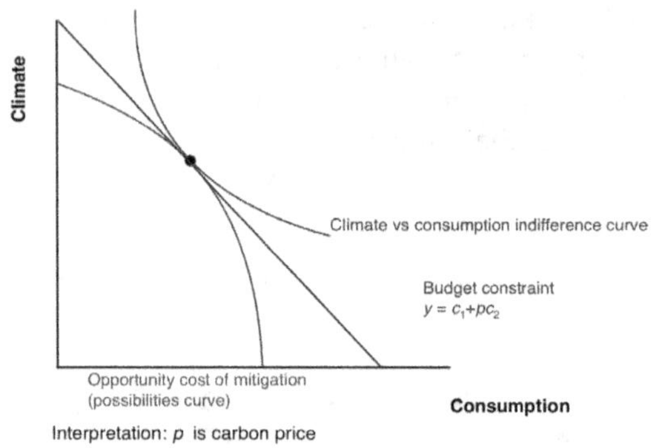

The Fundamental Diagram: Climate

Why Doesn't This Happen?

- Climate is a global public good:
  - non-excludable and non-rival,
  - free rider problem.
- Carbon prices are politically problematic:
  - easier to get voter support for less efficient, but more direct policies, such as subsidies for renewables,
  - economists aren't very good policy advocates.

What to Do?

- Instead of creating a market price, set the quantity.
- Carbon budget should be set.
- The amount of CO_2 that can be emitted should be consistent with some given probability of limiting global warming to a specified "safe" level.
- 450 ppm, 50 percent chance 2 degrees, 2900 $GtCO_2$-e (more details on this later if there is time).
- Paris Agreement (Intended) Nationally Determined Contribution should be ensured.

The Opportunity Cost of Emissions with a Fixed Budget

- Given a global or national carbon budget, total quantity of emissions is fixed.
- A tonne of emissions generated for one purpose is a tonne of emissions that must be reduced elsewhere if the budget constraint is to be met.
- Opportunity cost is always relevant.

Opportunity Cost is Still Crucial

- Every choice comes at the cost of the next-best alternative.
- This comes with or without (explicit) prices and markets.
- **Price–quantity duality:** A fixed quantity implicitly determines a price and vice versa.
- **Shadow price:** This includes the value of relaxing a constraint.

Allocating the Budget

The subsequent sections discuss the following:

- electricity,
- transport,
- other energy uses,
- land use,
- other greenhouse gases.

Electricity

- This is a comparatively easy one.
- Focus on energy efficiency is key.
- New renewables (solar PV and wind) already prove to be the cheapest options for new generation.
- Storage including batteries and pumped hydro can be considered.
- Solar thermal and geothermal energy are still in contention.
- Other also-rans include nuclear (fission and fusion), carbon capture, and sequestration.

Transport

- Distance travelled is still increasing, but more slowly in developed countries.
- Fuel efficiency is key for internal combustion engines.
- Another also-ran includes alternative fuels.
- Electric vehicles highlight the following features:
  - benefits depend on decarbonizing electricity supply;
  - becoming cost-competitive;
  - need infrastructure investment.

Industrial Use

- Direct combustion of carbon-based fuels to refine metals, produce steel, concrete and more.
- Mitigation options include new production processes, recycling of scrap, alternative materials.
- This is likely to entail the highest mitigation costs.

Land Use and Agriculture

- Low-cost options include the following:
  - reduced land clearing and reafforestation (net benefits in many cases when local environmental benefits are considered),
  - improved practices in paddy rice.
- Emissions from ruminants bring focus on the following:
  - feed supplements,
  - capture,
  - eating different.

Time and the Carbon Budget

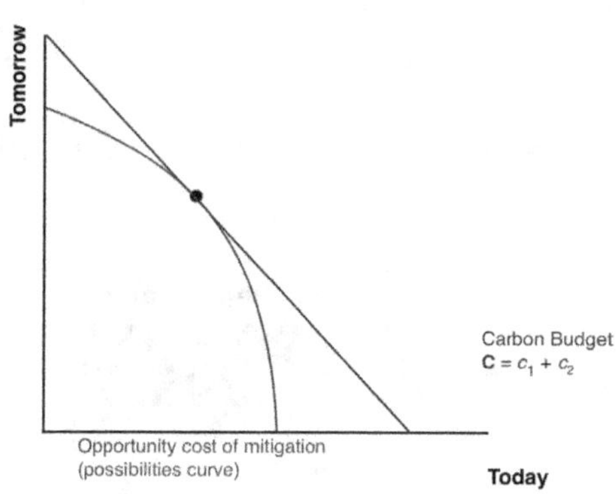

Interpretation: all emissions are equal, $p = 1$

A Simple Emissions Trajectory

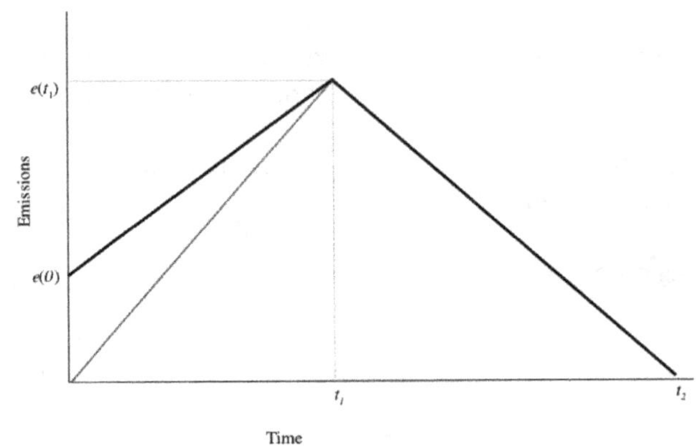

Implied Decarbonization Date for 450 ppm Target

	Peak year			
Emissions growth rate	2020	2025	2030	2035
0.5	2070	2062	2055	2049
0.75	2066	2057	2050	2044
1	2063	2053	2046	2040
1.5	2057	2047	2040	***
2	2052	2043	2036	***

Can We Get There?

- If emissions decline over 2020s, decarbonization is complete by 2050.
- Emissions seem broadly stable since 2014, but likely to increase with economic recovery from COVID-19.
- There is widespread agreement on the goal of 2050 decarbonization.
- But policies are not yet there.

Holding Heating to 1.5 degrees

- This seems a lot more difficult.
- This will probably require negative net emissions after 2050.
- Trees or new technology are needed to remove CO_2 from the atmosphere.
- Methane will gradually decline if emissions are stopped.

Lecture 5

Opportunity Cost and Market Failure

In this lecture, the concept of social opportunity cost is used to develop the idea of 'market failure'. In an ideal competitive equilibrium, private and social opportunity costs are equal to each other and to market prices. But, economic outcomes are rarely ideal.

The lecture begins by restating the two lessons:

Lesson 1: Market prices reflect and determine opportunity costs faced by consumers and producers.

Lesson 2: Market prices don't reflect all the opportunity costs we face as a society. Lesson 2 delves into the limitations of market prices in accounting for broader societal opportunity costs. It encompasses instances where market prices fail to capture externalities, public goods, and other factors that affect the well-being of society beyond individual transactions. Market failure occurs when these external costs or benefits are not internalized within the price mechanism, leading to inefficient resource allocation. Examples include situations where markets for certain goods or services do not exist or function poorly, macroeconomic failures, and issues related to income distribution. Government intervention or policy measures are often required to correct market failures and promote social welfare.

These two lessons highlight the dual role of market prices: They efficiently allocate resources at the microeconomic level (Lesson 1) while potentially falling short in capturing all relevant opportunity costs at the macroeconomic and societal levels (Lesson 2). Recognizing and addressing these market failures is crucial for achieving both efficiency and equity in economic systems.

Divergences between private and social opportunity costs are often called 'market failures' because they arise from malfunctioning or absent markets. The term 'imperfections' is also used, reflecting the fact that markets are not perfectly competitive. But, this term, implicitly treating market failures like superficial blemishes on an otherwise perfect piece of fruit, is misleading. As the example of climate change shows, market failures are pervasive and large in scale.

We first consider the following standard examples of market failure, drawing on the pioneering work of Francis Bator:

- Monopoly/monopsony;
- Oligopoly/oligopsony;
- Information asymmetries: adverse selection and moral hazard;
- Externalities;
- Public goods.

All of these are important, but the two examples most relevant to the problem of climate change are externalities and public goods. Climate change may be considered an externality because individual and corporate emissions of greenhouse gases harm everyone else. Alternatively, we may consider the atmosphere as a global good and emissions of greenhouse gases as actions which degrade that public good.

Whether we view climate change in terms of externalities or public goods, there is a divergence between private and social opportunity cost, that is, a market failure. Indeed, Sir Nicholas Stern has described climate change as 'the greatest market failure in history'.

The externality idea began with discussions of economies of scale in production. These were separated into internal economies (those achieved by increasing production within a firm) and external economies (those arising when firms cluster together, now often called economies of agglomeration). But, over time, attention was shifted to negative externalities, particularly those arising from pollution. Initially, these were mostly local and unilateral (as with smoke from factories), but over time they extended across borders (as with acid rain) and then became global and reciprocal (climate change, where nearly everyone contributes to the problem, and suffers from it, though in different degrees).

Whenever an externality exists, prices differ from opportunity costs. This means there is a free lunch left on the table. In principle at least, the externality can be corrected in a way that makes everyone better off.

The obvious solution to a divergence between prices and opportunity costs is a tax or subsidy that eliminates the gap. This solution is called Pigovian, after the great British economist AC Pigou. It will be discussed in more detail in Lecture 10.

Pigovian taxes are not the only solution. Framing the problem in terms of market failure leads to the idea of creating the missing markets, which in turn requires the creation of property rights to be traded in those markets. This was the great insight of British-born Chicago economist Ronald Coase, and has been reflected in the creation of markets in tradable emission permits, also discussed further in Lecture 10.

Thinking about global heating as an externality points in the direction of carbon pricing and emission permits. By contrast, thinking about the atmosphere as a global public good points in the direction of public investment in clean energy. The standard definition of a public good states that it is non-rival (use by one person doesn't affect its use by others) and non-excludable (if it is available to one person, it is available to everybody).

I illustrate the distinction between non-rivalry and non-excludability using a classic of Australian children's literature, *The Magic Pudding*. The titular character is a bad-tempered pudding on legs, called Albert, with the magical power to 'cut and come again'. If a slice is cut from the pudding (you can pick whatever flavor of pudding) you like, it instantly regrows.

The pudding is perfectly non-rival, but also perfectly excludable (if it can be caught). The plot of the story hinges on the theft of the pudding by villains seeking to control an unlimited supply of desserts and the efforts of the heroes to rescue (or perhaps recapture) it.

The global atmosphere in its natural state clearly meets the standard criteria for a public good. The air is free for all to breathe. And, as the Australian–New Zealand rock band *Crowded House* memorably put it, 'Everywhere you go you always take the weather with you'.

However, public goods can be degraded by uses that do not satisfy these conditions. Polluting the atmosphere changes the weather and imposes costs on everyone. And, given the limited capacity of the atmosphere to absorb greenhouse gases, reflected in the carbon budget, the non-rivalry condition also ceases to apply.

The lecture concludes with a discussion of the relationship between the Two Lessons and the mixed economy. Markets are essential for aligning prices with opportunity costs, shifting resources from less valued to more valued uses, and enabling the efficient allocation of goods and services. Nevertheless, market failures, such as externalities and information gaps, are pervasive. These market failures necessitate a robust state presence.

A crucial example of this need is the challenge of global heating. Both markets and state action are needed for an effective response.

Reading

Quiggin, J. (2019) *Economics in Two Lessons: Why Markets Work so Well, and Why they can Fail so Badly*. Princeton UP, Princeton, NJ (Chapter 10).

The Two Lessons Again

- **Lesson 1:** Market prices reflect and determine opportunity costs faced by consumers and producers.
- **Lesson 2:** Market prices don't reflect all the opportunity costs we face as a society.

Opportunity Cost and Market Failure

- Market failure covers instances of Lesson 2 where the divergence arises from the non-existence or poor function of a market for some good or service.
- Other instances of Lesson 2 include macroeconomic failures and inequitable income distribution.

Imperfections

- Market failures are sometimes described as "imperfections" similar to superficial blemishes on an otherwise perfect piece of fruit.
- But markets are far from perfect.
- Equilibrium under perfect competition provides a useful benchmark but no more.

Standard Examples of Market Failure

- monopoly/monopsony;
- oligopoly/oligopsony;
- information asymmetries: adverse selection and moral hazard;
- externalities;
- public goods.

Externalities

- Production and consumption activities that affect people other than the producers and consumers concerned.
- Most important negative externalities arise from pollution, e.g., global heating.
- Positive externality: A more educated population benefits everyone (we hope!).

Externalities are Pervasive

- This is more so, particularly in relation to climate.
- Almost everything we do in markets, as consumers, workers and business owners, affects people other than those with whom we transact directly.
- Every use of energy affects the amount of CO_2 in the atmosphere:
  - In the absence of active public policy, we would be overwhelmed by air and water pollution along with many other externalities.
  - US Senator Sheldon Whitehouse said in 2013: "We pay for power plant pollution through higher health costs."

Externalities: Etymology

- **Origin:** Distinction between "internal" and "external" economies of scale;
- **Internal economies of scale:** Firms with larger output have lower unit costs:
  - larger boilers and furnaces are more efficient.
  - Fixed inputs and "overhead" costs can be spread across more units of output.
- **External economies of scale:** The greater the total industry output, the lower the costs of each firm:
  - larger supply of skilled workers;
  - networks of input suppliers;
  - consumers know where to look.

Pigou on Externalities

- See Economics of Welfare (1920).
- He extended the idea of externalities.
- He noted divergences of market prices and social opportunity costs.
- He proposed a remedy: Pigouvian taxes.

Classification

- Unilateral:
  - actions of one party affect others;
  - air pollution from a factory.
- Bilateral:
  - interactions between neighbors.
- Congestion:
  - many users of an asset degrade its usefulness.
- Network:
  - positive externalities from more users — social networks.

Implications

- If a good generates negative externalities in production or consumption, prices differ from opportunity costs.
- Free lunch is left on the table.
- This can make everyone better off, but should we?
- Compared to what baseline?

Baseline: Existing Pollution

- This ignores externality.
- Opportunity cost of reducing pollution is lower output.
- At the margin, assuming profit maximization, MC = *P*.
- Loss in profit for a marginal change in output is zero.
- Opportunity cost of a small reduction in output is less than the benefit of lower pollution.
- We can, if we choose, subsidize existing polluters to reduce output and get a free lunch:
  - Should we do this?

Baseline: Zero Production

- Suppose some level of production is essential.
- More precisely, marginal value at zero exceeds social opportunity cost, including pollution externality.
- If we can make producers compensate those affected, we can get a free lunch.

Pigou's Solution

- Impose a tax on production equal to the difference between private and social opportunity costs at the margin.
- If the tax rate is set correctly, there are no free lunches left on the table in equilibrium.
- Whether we get a free lunch relative to a baseline depends on how revenue is distributed.

Coase and Property Rights

- Don't worry about government intervention.
- Rules about pollution imply an allocation of property rights.
- If parties can negotiate, they will make a mutually beneficial bargain.
- No free lunches.

Choice of Baseline is Critical

- Zero baseline implies property rights to clean air:
  - Polluters must pay those affected enough to compensate them for damage.
  - Compare 'offsets' for land development, etc.
- Status quo baseline implies rights to pollute:
  - Those affected must pay polluters to stop.
  - This could be implemented by creating tradable pollution permits and giving them to polluters.
  - Problem: Give permits to existing polluters or everyone who might want to undertake a polluting activity.

Allocation Rules Matter

- Grandfathering:
  - Give rights to existing polluters.
    - Origin is the "grandfather clause" used to suppress Blacks in the US south.
    - You can only vote if your grandfather was entitled to vote.
    - If polluters anticipate the creation of "grandfathered" rights, they may increase output to secure more rights.
- Give rights to everybody:
  - Effects similar to a Pigouvian tax.
  - Existing polluters must buy rights from others.

Public Goods

- non-rival, non-excludable;
- free rider problem;
- voluntary contributions;
- multiple interactions and repeated games.

Non-Rival

- Use by one person doesn't affect availability to others.
- Opportunity cost of consumption is zero.
- Information is a non-rival good.
- Other examples include Internet and national defense.

Non-Excludable

- No (cost-effective) way of restricting use to a particular group.
- Broadcast TV and unfenced parks.
- Information can be made excludable through secrecy or intellectual property (patents and copyright):
  - But this is socially costly.

The Magic Pudding

The *Magic Pudding* is a classic Australian children's book by Norman Lindsay. As explained in the notes, the pudding is an example of a good that is non-rival but excludable.

Paying for Public Goods

- Standard answer is public provision:
  - Avoids free-rider problems.
- But with small numbers and repeated interaction, voluntary provision may be adequate:
  - Especially with multiple goods and heterogeneous preferences.
  - I contribute to your preferred good if you contribute to mine.

Global Public Goods

- Global aspects of the environment:
  - atmosphere;
  - biodiversity;
- (Avoidance of) pandemic disease;
- (For altruists) general wellbeing of humanity.

Not the Only Market Failures

- monopoly;
- asymmetric information;
- unemployment and recession;
- income distribution and distributional conflict.

Two Lessons and the Mixed Economy

- Markets perform a vital role in matching prices and opportunity costs:
  - Shifting resources from less to more valued uses.
- But, market failures are pervasive:
  - A large and strong state is needed if markets are to work well.
- Global heating is a crucial example.

Lecture 6

The Emissions Equation

This lecture begins with the emissions equation, an arithmetic identity relating carbon emissions (C) to energy use (E), energy services (S), and aggregate output (G). The equation takes the form

$$C = C/E * E/S * S/G * G.$$

To reduce emissions, it is necessary either to reduce one of the three ratios — C/E (carbon intensity of energy), E/S (inverse of energy efficiency), or S/G (energy service share of GDP) — or to reduce GDP. We discuss options for each of these in turn.

Reducing the ratio of carbon emissions (C) to energy use (E) is a crucial aspect of mitigating climate change and transitioning to a sustainable future. Several strategies can be employed to achieve this reduction. Most strategies begin with shifting to cleaner sources, like renewables and potentially nuclear power, to decarbonize electricity production. Given a decarbonized electricity supply, the transition from internal combustion vehicles to electric ones in the transportation sector and in industries can further reduce emissions. Clean electricity can also be used to produce hydrogen, which has a wide range of potential uses. Industrial processes currently using coal and gas can then be replaced with electricity and hydrogen. Most notably, the use of blast furnaces to produce steel can be replaced by a combination of direct reduction of iron (DRI), using hydrogen, and recycling of scrap steel in electric arc furnaces.

However, this transition carries costs, including the early scrapping and replacement of carbon-intensive assets, such as coal-fired power stations.

Technological innovation, robust research and development, and global cooperation are necessary to achieve meaningful decarbonization and address climate change effectively.

Reducing energy use (E) relative to energy services (S) or, in other words, improving energy efficiency typically requires an upgrade of capital stock, replacing older, less efficient equipment and infrastructure with more energy-efficient alternatives. Examples includes replacing incandescent bulbs with LED light bulbs, upgrading household appliances, adopting more efficient industrial techniques, and transitioning to energy-efficient motor vehicles.

While there is a higher capital cost associated with acquiring energy-efficient technologies and equipment, these investments are typically offset by savings in energy costs over time and by reductions in carbon emissions. Evaluating the trade-offs involved here requires the use of discounting methods.

Reducing (S/G) involves replacing energy-intensive goods and services with less energy-intensive alternatives. For instance, favoring communications over physical transport can reduce the energy intensity associated with travel. Similarly, promoting remote working can lower the energy footprint associated with daily commuting.

Prioritizing experiences over the acquisition of physical goods can also contribute to energy savings. Experiences often have a lower energy footprint than the production and transportation of consumer goods. Opting for local 'staycations' instead of overseas travel can significantly cut down on energy-intensive international flights and accommodations. This shift benefits local economies while reducing the environmental impact of long-distance travel.

While these strategies offer energy savings, they may come with adjustment costs and, in some cases, potential utility losses for consumers.

Finally, we consider the concept of 'degrowth', which arises in many discussions about sustainable economic and environmental practices. In a fixed-proportions economy, where proportional relationships between carbon emissions (C), energy use (E), energy services (S), and aggregate output (G) cannot be altered, the link between emissions (C) and economic growth (G) is rigid.

In this scenario, any reduction in emissions (C) can only be achieved by decreasing overall economic activity (G). This prospect of degrowth is embraced by some advocates of a 'simple life' and sustainable living, who see it as a way to reduce the social and environmental harms of a consumption-driven society. However, it is met with resistance from opponents of climate action who fear potential economic repercussions.

It is important to note that the real-world economy is not of fixed proportions, and we have alternative strategies at our disposal beyond degrowth. However, some versions of degrowth seem likelier to be welcomed by many. For example, shorter working hours may be achieved through a reduction in standard weekly hours, as in recent proposals for a four-day working week, or through increases in holidays and leave.

We also consider a range of policy options to improve the ratios that drive the emissions equation. 'No regrets' policies are those that have positive outcomes regardless of the severity of climate change, making them attractive options. Explicitly price-based policies put a cost on carbon emissions, such as carbon taxes or cap-and-trade systems, incentivizing emission reduction. Implicitly price-based policies, on the other hand, encourage carbon reduction indirectly, often through subsidies and incentives for clean practices.

Regulations set specific requirements and standards for emissions, energy efficiency, and environmental protection. Public investment involves governments funding research and sustainable infrastructure, while promoting technological innovation encourages the development and deployment of clean technologies.

Summing up, it is essential to reduce a combination of factors, including the carbon intensity of energy (C/E), energy efficiency (E/S), energy intensity of output (S/G), and output growth (G). These variables are interconnected, and the opportunity cost of neglecting one is the need to intensify efforts on the others. It is important to avoid an excessive focus on a single parameter as this may lead to a misallocation of effort. The principle of opportunity cost is crucial here.

Readings

Australian Conservation Foundation (2010) Better Than Growth. https://d3n8a8pro7vhmx.cloudfront.net/auscon/pages/1358/attachments/original/1474590438/ACF_Better_Than_Growth_2010_11.pdf.

Rockstrom, J. *et al.* (2017) A roadmap for rapid decarbonization. *Science*, **355**, 1269, http://science.sciencemag.org/content/355/6331/1269.abstract.

The Emissions Equation Explains How Emissions are Determined by a Multi-stage Process

- $C = C/E * E/S * S/G * G$.
  - C = carbon emissions;
  - E = energy use;
  - S = energy services;
  - G = GDP.
- C/E is the carbon intensity of energy.
- E/S is the inverse of energy efficiency.
- S/G is the energy service share of GDP.

All Emissions are Equal

- That is, all emissions are equally bad.
- As far as climate is concerned, one CO_2 molecule is the same as another.
- It doesn't matter what activity generates emissions.
- It doesn't matter where emissions take place.
- It doesn't matter (much) when emissions take place — effects are almost permanent.

Costs and Benefits of Mitigation

- **Opportunity cost:** The cost is the next best alternative.
- The best alternative to mitigation is adaptation:
  - Accept that global heating is going to happen and live with it.
- Some heating is inevitable, so the choice is between mitigation + some adaptation and adaptation only.

Opportunity Costs

- We need to reduce some combination of carbon intensity of energy (*C/E*), energy efficiency (*E/S*), energy intensity of output (*S/G*), and output growth (*G*).
- The opportunity cost of doing less on one of these variables is the need to do more on others.
- Excessive focus on one parameter may be misleading.

Reducing *C/E*

- 'Decarbonizing' energy supply:
- **Electricity:** Replace coal with gas, coal and gas with renewables (or nuclear?).
- **Transport:** Replace internal combustion with electricity.
- **Other industrial uses:** Replace coal and gas with electricity, hydrogen, etc.

Costs of Decarbonization: General

- This involves replacing existing capital stock ("stranded assets").
- Higher operating costs can be noted in some cases: the need for technological innovations.

Cost of Decarbonization: Electricity

- For the new generation, the cost of decarbonization is zero or negative: Unsubsidized PV and wind are cheaper than fossil fuels, even with storage costs for firming.
- To replace existing capacity, costs depend on the following:
  - age and efficiency of existing carbon-burning plants;
  - fuel prices (no world market for gas);
  - valuation of health effects (justifies shutdown of nearly all existing coal);
  - speed at which new plants can be constructed.

Cost of Decarbonization: Transport

- Electrification requires decarbonization of generation.
- This requires new investment in charging infrastructure.
- This involves early scrapping of the existing ICE fleet.
- Higher capital costs are offset by lower running costs: discounting.
- Air transport remains problematic.

Cost of Decarbonization: Industrial Uses

- This varies from case to case, depending on alternative technology.
- **Aluminum**: Mainly electricity.
- **Steel**: DRI (using hydrogen) + recycling.
- **Cement**: Low-carbon technologies under development.

Reducing *E/S*: Energy Efficiency

- Replace existing capital stock with more efficient alternatives:
  - incandescent to LED light bulbs;
  - appliances;
  - industrial techniques;
  - motor vehicles.
- Higher capital cost offset by savings in energy cost:
  - discounting, again.

Reducing *S/G*: Energy Intensity

- Substitute less energy-intensive goods and services for more:
  - communications instead of transport;
  - remote working;
  - warm/cool clothes instead of heating and air conditioning;
  - experiences instead of physical goods;
  - local "staycations" instead of overseas travel.
- Energy savings but adjustment costs, possible utility losses.

Reducing *G*: Aggregate Output

- Shorter working hours:
  - standard weekly hours;
  - holidays and leave;
  - retirement age.
- Continued technological progress, so not a stationary economy.

Public Policy Options

- "no regrets" (free lunch) policies;
- explicitly price-based policies;
- implicitly price-based policies;
- regulation;
- public investment;
- technological innovation.

"No Regrets" Policies

- improvement without opportunity cost;
- more broadly, policies with net benefits even at a carbon price of zero;
- missed opportunities for energy efficiency (*E/S*);
- ending local pollution from coal and oil (*C/E*): coal-fired power stations, ICE vehicles, etc.;
- congestion pricing for roads (*S/G*).

Explicitly Price-based Policies

- Carbon tax:
  - This is also known as the Pigouvian tax.
  - Tax rate is set equal to marginal social damage.
  - The market will work out the optimal level of emissions.
- Emissions trading scheme:
  - This is inspired by Coase.
  - This helps determine the target level of emissions and create corresponding permits.
  - The market determines the price.

Grandfathering

- This has already been discussed in Lecture 5.
- This allocates rights to existing polluters.
- This is often associated with emissions trading, but not necessarily.
- We can use auctions with emissions trading schemes, with no grandfathering.
- "Baseline and credit" carbon tax schemes create grandfathering.

Implicitly Price-based Policies

- Renewable energy target:
  - Retailers must source a proportion of electricity from renewables.
  - Tradeable certificates work like emissions permits.
- Emissions reduction fund:
  - This includes tenders to reduce emissions.
  - The problems of additionality, compliance, etc. come into focus.

Regulation (Mostly *C/E*, *E/S*)

- energy efficiency standards for buildings and appliances;
- vehicle fuel efficiency mandates;
- "direct action";
- significant but hidden opportunity costs;
- works well when market incentives work badly: long-lived capital items where energy savings hard to measure.

Public Investment

- Specific investments in emissions-reducing initiatives include Horndale big battery (SA), Snowy 2.0 (Cwlth), CleanCo (Qld), and car-charging networks.
- Under public ownership, investments are directed to reduce emissions.
- Carbon pricing is integrated into public investment decisions in general (the US has a price of $38/tonne).

Technological Innovation

- **Electricity:** Solar PV, wind, and batteries delivering cheap, clean power:
  - (mostly) failed hopes: nuclear, carbon capture & sequestration, geothermal;
  - given multiple options, good chance that at least one will work.
- **Transport:** Electric cars vs public transport, telecommuting.
- **Hydrogen and ammonia**: Complementary to renewable electricity.
- **Steel**: Shift to direct reduced iron now accelerating.
- **Cement and other industrial options**: Still looking for tech solutions.

National Technology Policies

- Germany Energiewende (transition):
  - shift from coal + nuclear to renewables
    - did this in the wrong order.
    - relied too much on (mostly Russian) gas;
  - support for solar catalysts for dramatic cost reductions;
  - lots of adjustment assistance.
- Australia technology roadmap:
  - "stretch goals" for cost reductions in CCS, hydrogen, etc.;
  - mismatch between ambition of goals and limited/symbolic funding.

Civil Society

- Non-government organizations, businesses, unions, churches, other associations.
- **Divestment**: Financial institutions stop investing in, financing, and insuring projects based on coal, oil, and gas.
- **Green bans** (most prevalent in the 1970s): Unions refusing to work on environmentally destructive projects.
- **NGOs**: Local resistance to destructive projects, advocacy of public policies.

Individual Action

- Modest lifestyle changes such as recycling and turning off lights:
  - This is arguably a substitute for political action.
- Radical lifestyle changes such as veganism, going off-grid, and minimizing vehicle use:
  - Not many people are willing/able to adopt the full package.

Degrowth

- In a fixed-proportions economy, we can't change C/E, E/S, S/G.
- C (emissions) is directly proportional to G (aggregate output).
- We can only reduce C by reducing G.
- This prospect has been welcomed by some advocates of "simple life" but also feared by the opponents of climate action.
- But the economy isn't fixed-proportions and we have options other than degrowth.

Lecture 7

Discounting, Distribution, and Uncertainty

Action (or inaction) on climate change has different effects:

now and in the future;

on different people at any point in time; and

in different possible futures.

All of these different effects involve trade-offs, and all can be analyzed using the concept of opportunity cost. Indeed, they can all be analyzed using the same simple diagram used in an Economics 101 course to illustrate choices between two different consumer goods, such as movie tickets and T-shirts.

In this lecture, the point is demonstrated with three diagrams, or rather the same diagram with four different sets of labels. The first box on "Discounting, Distribution and Uncertainty" is the standard model of consumer and producer choice for with a single individual (in Economics 101, commonly referred to as 'Robinson Crusoe', after the fictional character marooned on an island and initially alone).

There are two goods, fish and fruit. The more effort Crusoe spends catching fish, the less he can spend picking fruit. The convex red curve represents the combinations of fish and fruit Crusoe can gather in the time available.

The downward slope reflects the opportunity cost trade-off between fishing time and fruit-picking time.

The fact that the curve is convex reflects diminishing marginal productivity. Crusoe starts by picking the 'low-hanging fruit', which doesn't require much effort and therefore doesn't take much time away from fishing. As Crusoe picks more fruit, it becomes harder to get and the opportunity cost, in terms of fish, is higher. This opportunity cost may be expressed in terms of the marginal rate of transformation in production.

Crusoe's choices will depend on his preferences. These are represented by the 'indifference curve' in blue, which shows combinations of fruit and fish that Crusoe regards as equally desirable. More fruit compensates for less fish and vice versa. The pale blue line, which is everywhere above the production possibilities curve, also shows equally desirable combinations of fish and fruit, but these aren't feasible given the natural resources and technology available to Crusoe.

Symmetrically, with the case of production possibilities, the concavity of the indifference curve represents the changing marginal rate of substitution in consumption . The more fruit Robinson eats, the less he values an additional piece and the more he would give up for an additional fish.

The point E (for equilibrium) where the red and blue curves touch (or, if you prefer Latinate expressions, the point of tangency) represents the highest level of satisfaction Robinson can obtain with the available resources and technology. The crucial requirement is that the marginal rate of substitution in consumption (the amount of fruit Robinson would give up for an extra fish) should equal the marginal rate of transformation (the fruit Robinson could pick in the time taken to catch the extra fish).

We can take this a bit further by considering a large economy in which Robinson is an average or 'representative' producer and consumer. The red curve now represents the aggregate production possibilities for the economy and the indifference curve is a representation of average preferences over fish and fruit. In a market economy, the two goods will be traded at a price determined by opportunity costs in production and by consumer preferences. Relative prices may be represented by a line indicating quantities of fish and fruit that have the same market value, colored green in the figure.

If markets are competitive, and everyone is well informed, equilibrium prices will yield the equilibrium quantity derived previously. At this price, the people in the economy considered producers will maximize the value of their output by producing E. Similarly, considered as consumers, they will achieve the highest level of satisfaction, consistent with spending the value of their output.

At the ideal equilibrium, the price of fruit, expressed in terms of fish, should be equal to both the marginal rate of substitution and the marginal rate of transformation.

All of this ought to be familiar (if only vaguely recalled) for anyone who has done an elementary economics course. And, for some students, it may seem obvious to the point of tedium.

I've gone through it in a lot of detail because the same exact diagram, with appropriate relabeling, can be used to understand more complex problems involving time, uncertainty, and distribution, all of which arise in relation to global heating.

The simplest relabeling is to replace the labels 'fish' and 'fruit' with 'goods' and 'environmental services', respectively. All production of goods requires natural resources as inputs. And, unless we take specific action to prevent or offset damage, giving up some goods we could otherwise consume, extraction and use of natural resources involve some loss of environmental services. So, the opportunity cost of more goods is less environmental services.

The choices we face here are similar to those between fish and fruit. But, because environmental services are public goods, markets do not emerge spontaneously to produce prices, and there is no reason to expect an optimal equilibrium. Such equilibrium can emerge if governments create the necessary markets, for example, emission markets for carbon dioxide. Ideally, these markets would be designed to move the economy to the equilibrium point E.

Next, let's consider choices over time. As we decide how to respond to global heating, we face choices between acting now to reduce emissions or waiting for later, with the result that we will incur more climate damage and need to spend more on mitigation and adaptation in the future. For example, we can close coal-fired power stations now and replace them carbon-free generation. Alternatively, we can let the power stations run until the end of their normal operating lives. This choice will imply more climate damage and a need for more radical mitigation options in the future.

We can represent these choices in the same two-dimensional diagram. The horizontal axis now represents consumption of goods and environmental services in the present. The vertical axis represents consumption in the future. As before, the production possibility curve determines the choice set.

The price line in the diagram now represents the rate of interest. With an interest rate r, the opportunity cost of a dollar of consumption today is $1 + r$ dollars in the future. Conversely, the opportunity cost of a dollar of consumption in the future is $1/(1 + r)$ dollars today. The interest rate is normally positive, reflecting the facts that (i) current investments yield a positive return after repaying the initial outlay and (ii) with rising incomes the marginal value of consumption is higher today than in the future.

The diagram has one additional feature. The diagonal line through the origin represents outcomes where consumption in the future is the same as in the present. Points above the line represent the usual case (at least until now) where living standards improve over time. Points below the line are those with declining living standards, implying that our present consumption patterns are unsustainable.

Now, consider the issue of income distribution. We can relabel the axes again, with 'poor' people (those with low market incomes) on the horizontal axis and 'rich' (high market incomes) on the vertical axis. Market income can be redistributed within countries through the tax and welfare system, and between countries through foreign aid. Such redistribution is costly; so, a transfer of one unit to the poor will reduce the net income of the rich by more than one unit. This is reflected in the term $(1 + \delta)$ in the budget constraint. The equilibrium outcome depends on social preference for equality and on the technology of redistribution.

Finally, what about uncertainty? The best way to think about uncertainty is to consider different possible future states of the world. In the context of climate change, we may consider 'good' states, where the sensitivity of global temperatures to CO_2 emissions is low, and 'bad' states, where sensitivity is high. Diverting investment to climate mitigation produces net benefits in bad states. In good states, the benefits of mitigation are less than the opportunity cost of forgoing investments in the production of market goods and services. The price in this case will depend on the relative probabilities of good and bad states, which can be measured as an odds ratio.

In the remainder of the lecture, the issues of discounting and uncertainty are spelled out in more detail. Sources of uncertainty in predicting the effects of global heating include model uncertainty, parameter uncertainty, emissions uncertainty, and uncertainty about damages. Last but not least is fabricated uncertainty, arising from the effects of climate science deniers and 'lukewarmers' who seek to slow down action to reduce emissions of greenhouse gases.

A crucial point in considering uncertainty, in relation to global heating and other issues, is that much of the expected damage is driven by relatively low-probability extreme events, sometimes referred to as 'tail risk'. This point is explained in some detail.

Readings

Quiggin, J. (2018) The importance of 'extremely unlikely' events: Tail risk and the costs of climate change. *Australian Journal of Agricultural and Resource Economics*, **62**, 4–20, http://dx.doi.org/10.1111/1467-8489.12238.

Weitzman, M. L. (2014) Fat tails and the social cost of carbon. *The American Economic Review*, **104**, 544–546, http://dash.harvard.edu/bitstream/handle/1/12992320/203061/aer.104.5.544fattailsandthesocialcostofcarbon.pdf?sequence=1.

Discounting, Distribution and Uncertainty

- Action (or inaction) on climate change has different effects:
  - now and in the future;
  - on different people at any point in time;
  - in different possible futures;
  - opportunity cost is the way to think about this.

Choice Between Goods

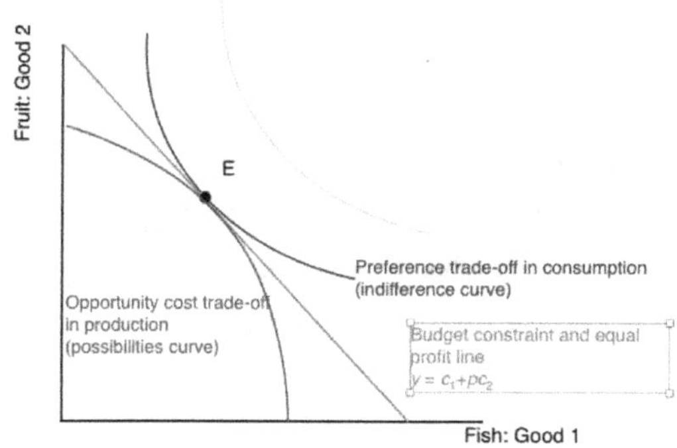

Market equilibrium: MRS = MRT = Price ratio

Social Choice and Time

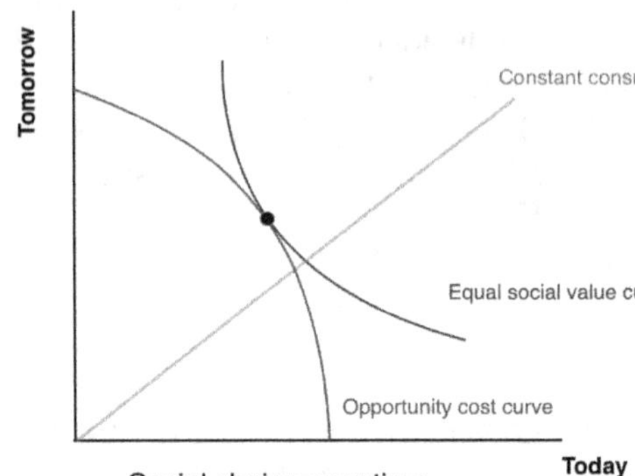

Social choice over time

Opportunity cost explains rising consumption and positive interest rates

Social Choice and Income Distribution

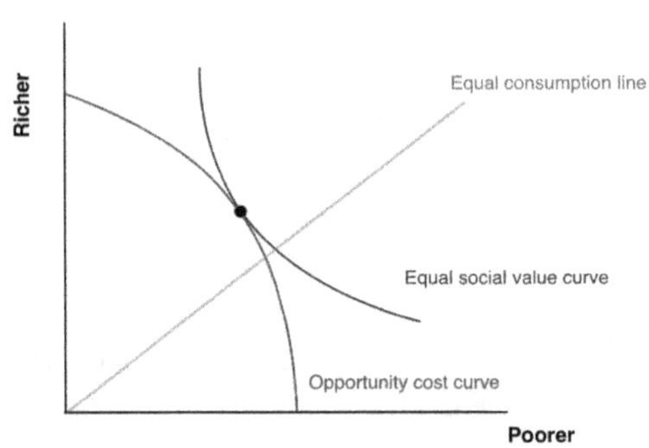

Social choice and income distribution

Opportunity cost explains costly redistribution

Social Choice, Risk and Uncertainty

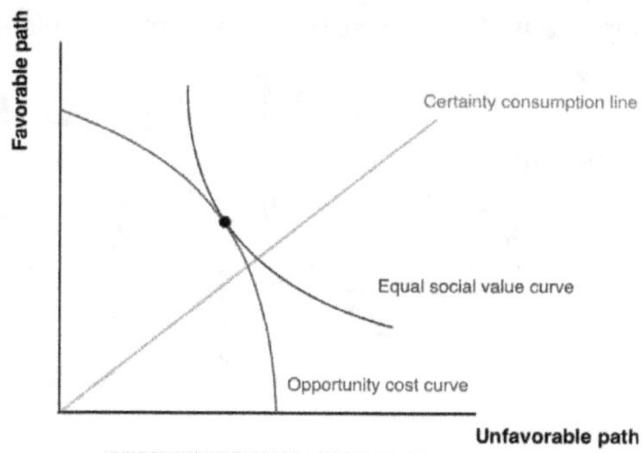

Social choice and uncertainty

Opportunity cost explains risk premium

Now and in the Future

- Opportunity cost of inaction today.
- Some combination of
  - more climate damage from now into the future;
  - more costly mitigation in the future.
- How should we compare current and future costs and benefits?

Investment and Discounting

- For market goods and services, giving up a unit of consumption today and investing yields more than one unit in the future.
- That is, the opportunity cost of a unit current consumption is greater than one unit of future consumption.

Discounting and the Environment

- In many cases, we will have less environmental services in the future than now:
  - climate change;
  - species extinction.
- So, the opportunity cost of environmental services will be higher in the future than today.

Current and Future Generations

- This is a common way of posing the problem, but a wrong one.
- Generations do not live at different points in time, they overlap.
- Today's children will (mostly) still be alive in 2100.
- Inherent discounting means discriminating against today's young people, not "future generations".

Winners and Losers

- Who gains and loses from climate policy depends critically on policy design.
- We want the burden to fall on those best able to bear it.
- Clean Energy Act:
  - fully (or more than fully) compensated low-income households;
  - but too many free carbon units (grandfathering).

Uncertainty and Confidence

- Uncertainty is typically defined over a well-defined range of possibilities:
    - which side of a die will end face up;
    - which horse will win the race;
    - may be expressed in terms of probabilities.
- Confidence is about how thoroughly we have examined the evidence and whether it is "conclusive".
- Benefit–cost analysis uses measures of uncertainty, and legal proceeding uses measures of confidence:
    - for example, beyond reasonable doubt.

IPCC Measure of Confidence

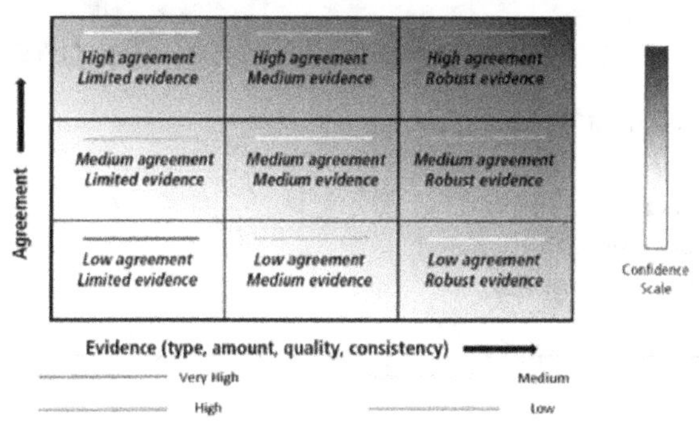

Figure 1: Confidence levels are a combination of level of agreement and evidence. There are five levels, shown with colours. (IPCC 2013)

Source: https://theconversation.com/lost-in-translation-confidence-and-certainty-in-climate-science-17181.

IPCC Likelihood

Table 1. Likelihood Scale	
Term*	**Likelihood of the Outcome**
Virtually certain	99-100% probability
Very likely	90-100% probability
Likely	66-100% probability
About as likely as not	33 to 66% probability
Unlikely	0-33% probability
Very unlikely	0-10% probability
Exceptionally unlikely	0-1% probability

Uncertainty About Global Heating

- model uncertainty;
- parameter uncertainty;
- emissions uncertainty;
- impacts uncertainty;
- fabricated uncertainty.

Model Uncertainty

- Models are always an approximation to the truth.
- Many different models of global climate exist.
- These include different drivers, different functional forms, solution procedures, and so on.
- Though there is a broad agreement on the trend, there are substantial differences.
- IPCC uses a "suite" of models to generate projections.

Emissions Uncertainty

- Most important input to any climate model is the time path of future emissions.
- This is the main variable we can actually control.
- Modelers use a variety of scenarios.

Impacts Uncertainty

- For a given change in climate, there is a lot of uncertainty about the damage (if any) it will cause.
- Issues include the following:
  - speed of adaptation;
  - value of natural ecosystems.
- Nordhaus, Stern, and others have tackled this.

Fabricated Uncertainty

- FUD refers to fear, uncertainty and doubt.
- This is used by climate science deniers.
- This is also used by "lukewarmers":
  - claim to accept mainstream science, but focus on the possibility that damage may be less than projected.

Parameter Uncertainty

- Within a given model, input parameters aren't known with certainty.
- Parameters are drawn from a complex joint distribution.
- Monte Carlo method takes lots of draws and plots the resulting distribution for variables of interest.
- Hsiang *et al*. use this for climate damage in the US.

Median and Tail

- Hsiang *et al*. focus on median values, and don't say much about right-hand tail.
- Median is around 3 degrees of warming:
  - damaging but bearable for the US.
- Right-hand tail is 8 degrees:
  - not properly modeled, almost certainly catastrophic.

Understanding Tail Probabilities

- Intergovernmental Panel on Climate Change (IPCC) uses probabilities to convey levels of scientific (un)certainty:
  - virtually certain = 99–100 percent probability;
  - very likely = 90–100 percent;
  - likely 66–100 percent;
  - about as likely as not = 33–66 percent;
  - unlikely = 0–33 percent;
  - very unlikely = 0–10 percent;
  - extremely unlikely 0–5 percent;
  - exceptionally unlikely = less than 1 percent.
- It is problematic when this terminology is used in risk analysis.

Risk Analysis Mostly Concerns "Extremely Unlikely" Events

- Examples are as follows:
  - 10-year risk of dying of lung cancer (for a 60-year-old smoker) 5 percent;
  - one-year risk of death from any cause (US) <1 percent;
  - 10-year risk of dying in a road crash (US) 0.1 percent;
  - flood control is based on the concept of a 100-year flood (1 percent annual).
- If we ignored extremely unlikely events, dangerous risks would look harmless.

Right-Hand Tail

- Note equilibrium warming above 6 °C.
- This is poorly represented in current models.
- This accounts for a large proportion of expected loss.

Why the Right-Hand Tail Matters

- Right-hand tail dominates for three reasons:
  - The higher the sensitivity, the greater the warming associated with additional emissions.
  - Since damage functions are convex, the greater the equilibrium warming, the greater the total and marginal damage associated with an additional degree of warming.
  - Since the utility of income is concave, the greater the damage associated with climate change, the greater the risk-adjusted present value of additional damage at the margin.

How Much Does the Right-Hand Tail Matter?

- Quiggin (2017):
  - Ignoring the upper tail of the distribution of possible outcomes will result in estimates of the social cost of CO_2 emissions that are less than half the correct value and sometimes much less than half.

A Unified Model

- expected utility model;
- time and discounting;
- expected utility and risk aversion;
- income distribution and egalitarianism.

The Expected Utility Model and Social Choice

- This maximizes expected utility for all people over time.
- This may assign different weights to different people and time periods:
  - But should we?
- The expected utility is the mean utility over all possible consumption paths.

The EU Formula

- $V = \Sigma_s \pi_s \Sigma_t \beta_t \Sigma_i w_i u(c_{sti})$:
  - C_{sti} is the consumption of person *i* at time *t* in path *s*.
  - *u* is the utility function.
  - w_i is the weight on person *I*.
  - B_t is the discount factor for time *t*.
  - π_s is the probability of path *s*.

Lecture 8

Wicked Problems

This lecture begins by comparing hard problems, impossible problems, and wicked problems.

Some problems are simply impossible. These are problems that, given our current knowledge and technology, cannot be solved. They lack feasible solutions within the known constraints. Economic analysis enables us to characterize some problems as impossible problems. Famous examples include the Arrow Impossibility Theorem in voting theory and the Mundell–Fleming Impossible Trinity in international monetary theory.

Comparing space travel and poverty eradication illustrates the concept of wicked problems. Space travel, while challenging, can be categorized as a 'hard problem' because it relies on well-established scientific principles and engineering solutions. Hard problems typically have clear solutions, even though the path to solving them may be complex.

In contrast, poverty eradication is a 'wicked problem' due to its multifaceted nature and the interplay of economic, social, political, and cultural factors. Poverty lacks a single, universally applicable solution and often demands complex, context-specific interventions.

Arguably, wicked problems are what's left after the easy problems and even the hard problems have been solved. They are characterized by a lack of clear problem boundaries, varying perspectives, and no single, definitive solution.

Wicked problems arise from the complexities of the modern world, including societal advancements, technological innovations, and globalization. As societies become more interconnected and interdependent, problems emerge that cannot be effectively addressed through traditional linear thinking or isolated expertise. Wicked problems blur the boundaries between disciplines and require collaborative, adaptive approaches to problem-solving.

There are a number of factors that tend to make problems 'wicked':

- When a problem has the potential to affect significant numbers of people with substantial gains or losses, it becomes politically charged and contentious.
- Wicked problems frequently arise from clashes between different cultural, social, and moral values. These conflicts can make it challenging to arrive at a consensus on how to address the problem.
- When economic conflicts intersect with cultural or social conflicts, the complexity of a problem intensifies. This interaction can lead to deeper divisions and make finding common ground even more difficult.
- Partisan political disputes over how to address wicked problems are increasingly common in countries like Australia and the United States. Polarization often hinders constructive dialogue and problem-solving.
- Wicked problems do not have a single source of disciplinary expertise that can define and understand the problem comprehensively. They require a multidisciplinary approach to account for various dimensions and perspectives.

There is a general distrust of experts and expertise, which can further complicate efforts to address wicked problems. This distrust can stem from political polarization, cultural divisions, or previous instances where expert advice was perceived as biased or ineffective.

Even compared to wicked problems in general, global heating stands out. Global heating is often referred to as a 'super-wicked problem' because it exhibits all the characteristics of a wicked problem, but with added urgency and unique challenges. It is a global issue with no central authority, interconnected with various other problems, such as energy policy, economics, and social equity. Moreover, the longer action is delayed, the more difficult and costly it becomes to mitigate its effects. Global heating embodies the essence of a wicked problem, demanding comprehensive, interdisciplinary solutions and rapid global cooperation.

What can be done about wicked and super-wicked problems? A number of approaches may be considered, addressing different aspects of these problems. Difficulties in modeling may be addressed through applied forward reasoning (Levin *et al*, Bernstein *et al*). Public understanding may be improved through better communication of the results of scientific research, through processes like the IPCC Assessment reports. Political actors can also build coalitions with the aim of locking in commitments to avoid backsliding in the future. The agreements made through the Conferences of Parties to the UN Framework Convention on Climate Change are one example.

Readings

Bernstein, S. *et al.* (2000) God gave Physics the easy problems: Adapting social science to an unpredictable world. *European Journal of International Relations*, **6**, 43–76.

Churchman, C. W. (1967) Guest editorial: Wicked problems. *Management Science*, **14**, B141–B142, https://www.jstor.org/stable/2628678.

Lazarus, R. J. (2008) Super wicked problems and climate change: Restraining the present to liberate the future. *Cornell Law Review*, **94**, 1153, http://scholarship.law.georgetown.edu/cgi/viewcontent.cgi?article=1152&context=facpub.

Levin, K. *et al.* (2009) Playing it forward: Path dependency, progressive incrementalism, and the "Super Wicked" problem of global climate change. *IOP Conference Series: Earth and Environmental Science*, **6**, 502002, http://dx.doi.org/10.1088/1755-1307/6/0/502002.

Levin, K. *et al.* (2012) Overcoming the tragedy of super wicked problems: Constraining our future selves to ameliorate global climate change. *Policy Sciences*, **45**, 123–152, http://dx.doi.org/10.1007/s11077-012-9151-0.

Rittel, H. & Webber, M. (1973) Dilemmas in a general theory of planning. *Policy Sciences*, **4**, 155–169, http://www.jstor.org/stable/4531523.

Weber, E. P. & Khademian, A. M. (2008) Wicked problems, knowledge challenges, and collaborative capacity builders in network settings. *Public Administration Review*, **68**, 334–349, http://frst411.sites.olt.ubc.ca/files/2015/01/25145606.pdf.

Problems

- Hard problems, impossible problems, and wicked problems: Space travel vs poverty eradication;
- Origin of the term;
- Climate change as a "super-wicked problem";
- Is communication a solution?
- Prospects for the future.

Going to the Moon: A Hard Problem

- US President John F Kennedy, responding to the first human space flight by Yuri Gagarin:
  - The USSR was then the major geostrategic rival of the US.
- It set the national goal of "landing a **man** on the Moon and returning him safely to the Earth" by the end of the 1960s:
  - The first woman in space was Valentina Tereshkova (USSR, 1963).
  - The second was Sally Ride (USA, 1983).
- We choose to go to the Moon in this decade not because it is easy, but because it is hard.

But Not a Wicked Problem

- Strong social consensus behind the goals of the project:
  - limited opposition based on concerns about failure to solve domestic problems:
    - opportunity cost reasoning, but only by a few.
- NASA engineers were the unchallenged source of expertise:
  - skills to solve problems of rocket design, take-off and landing, tracking, survival in space.
- Budgetary cost was substantial (peak of \$25 billion/year in current values) but manageable (roughly \$100/person/year for US population).

Interstellar Travel: An Impossible Problem

- **Space is big**. You just won't believe how vastly, hugely, mind-bogglingly **big** it **is**. — Douglas Adams, *The Hitchhiker's Guide to the Galaxy*.
- Speed of light is an absolute constraint:
  - Even hypothetical technologies involve 80-year round trips.
- With current technology, travel to the nearest star (apart from the Sun) would take 80,000 years.
  - No radical innovations could be seen since the 1970s.

Squaring the Circle

- Classical Greek mathematicians asked: Using only a straightedge and compass, can you construct a square with the same area as a given circle?
  - Professional and amateur mathematicians struggled with this over 2,000 years.
  - Many proposed solutions, but none were valid.
- *Modern formulation*: Is π an algebraic number (root of a polynomial with rational coefficients)? *Answer*: **No** (as proved by Lindeman in 1882).
- This is a metaphor for attempting the impossible.

Impossibility in Politics and Economics

- **Arrow Impossibility Theorem**: This takes a set of plausible conditions for a voting system and shows that no system satisfying these conditions can exist.
- **Mundell–Fleming Impossible Trinity**: This can't have
  - a fixed foreign exchange rate;
  - free capital movement (absence of capital controls);
  - an independent monetary policy.
- **Fiscal policy**: This can't have more spending, lower taxes, and smaller deficit.
- **Opportunity cost**: This is always relevant.

Impossible Problems are Solved Problems

- There is no longer a waste effort on futile goals.
- Impossibility results give us a deeper understanding of problems.
- Impossibilities enter correct problem formulation as constraints:
  - speed of light;
  - interest rate parity;
  - budget constraint.

A Wicked Problem: US War on Poverty

- This was launched by the US President Johnson in the 1960s.
- Major expansion of social welfare programs was
  - informed by the best available social science;
  - parallel with the Vietnam War (also failed).

Failure of the War on Poverty

- The war was abandoned by the Reagan Administration in the 1980s:
  - Was the war lost or did the government change sides?
- The US poverty rate has fluctuated over time, but there was no sustained fall:
  - an absolute poverty line based on the poverty level consumption in the 1960s.
- Other measures included declining life expectancy and deaths of despair.

What Went Wrong

- Cost constraints of two wars (Poverty and Vietnam) were ignored:
  - The opportunity cost of each was inadequate resources for the other.

No Agreement on Causes of Poverty

- moral character of poor;
- inadequate education;
- not enough money;
- interaction with cultural and racial conflict.

No Agreement on Solutions

- work vs welfare;
- education as a panacea;
- breakdown of full employment.

Wicked or Impossible?

- *The poor you will always have with you.*— Matthew 26:11
- Resource constraints aren't binding.
- Some poverty problems have been solved:
  - Poverty among the aged was largely eliminated in some European countries (though not in Australia).
  - Relative poverty was greatly reduced in mid-C20.

Origin of the Term

- Churchman (1967) attributes it to a suggestion made in a seminar by Horst Rittel (UC Architecture Department).
- The proposed definition included that class of social system problems that are ill-formulated, where the information is confusing, where there are many clients and decision makers with conflicting values, and where the ramifications in the whole system are thoroughly confusing. The adjective "wicked" is supposed to describe the mischievous and even evil quality of these problems, where proposed "solutions" often turn out to be worse than the symptoms.
- This was spelled out in more detail by Rittel and Webber (1973).

What Makes a Problem Wicked?

- There could be big gains and losses for large groups.
- Competing cultural/social values could be a problem.
- Interaction between economic and cultural conflicts makes things worse:
  - This is now the norm in Australian and US politics.
- There is no single source of disciplinary expertise to define and understand the problem:
  - general or issue-specific distrust of experts and expertise.

Interconnectedness

- Poverty is linked with education, nutrition with poverty, the economy with nutrition, and so on. These problems are typically offloaded to policy makers or are written off as being too cumbersome to handle *en masse*. Yet, these are the problems — poverty, sustainability, equality, and health and wellness — that plague our cities and our world and that touch each and every one of us (Kolko, https://ssir.org/articles/entry/wicked_problems_problems_worth_solving#).

What's Left After the Easy Problems and Even the Hard Problems Have Been Solved?

- The professional's job was once seen as solving an assortment of problems that appeared to be definable, understandable, and consensual.
- Record has been quite spectacular. The streets have been paved and roads now connect all places; houses shelter virtually everyone; the dreaded diseases are virtually gone; and so on.
- Nonetheless, the 1960s was a period of rising dissent and the rejection of professional authority in many fields.

Rittel and Webber

- Planning problems are "wicked".
- There is no definitive formulation of a wicked problem.
- Wicked problems have no stopping rule.
- Solutions to wicked problems are not true-or-false, but good-or-bad.
- There is no immediate and no ultimate test of a solution to a wicked problem.
- Every solution to a wicked problem is a "one-shot operation"; as there is no opportunity to learn by trial and error, every attempt counts significantly.

More on Wicked Problems

- Wicked problems do not have an enumerable (or an exhaustively describable) set of potential solutions, nor is there a well-described set of permissible operations that may be incorporated into the plan.
- Every wicked problem is essentially unique.
- Every wicked problem can be considered to be a symptom of another problem.
- The existence of a discrepancy representing a wicked problem can be explained in numerous ways. The choice of explanation determines the nature of the problem's resolution.
- The planner has no right to be wrong.

What To Do

- We need to act, even if there is no solution available:
  - Not to decide is to decide.
- This is an implication of opportunity cost reasoning.
- Partial solutions to subproblems:
  - This can address the health problems of poor families, even if poverty itself is intractable.
  - Problem of the second best: Local progress may make things worse overall.
- The core concept of incrementalism and "muddling through" (Lindblom, 1959) can be considered.

Climate Change as a Super-Wicked Problem

- Time is running out.
- There is no central authority.
- Those seeking to end the problem are also causing it.
- There is an intersection with cultural conflict.

Time is Running Out

- We should have started serious efforts in the 1990s.
- There is a need for complete decarbonization by 2050.
- This implies a reduction of 50 percent (on 2005 or similar baseline) by 2030.
- Long-lived capital investments are being made now.
- But putting off hard decisions is usually appealing.

No Central Authority

- There is a need for international coordination at a time of heightened conflict:
  - US vs China.
- There exists an unwillingness to accept binding international agreements:
  - fear of "world government".
- Corporations and sub-national governments are also important:
  - delaying mitigation: Exxon, Chinese provincial governments.
- Mitigation can be accelerated:
  - divestment by the financial sector, state governments in Australia and the US.

Those Seeking to End the Problem are Also Causing it

- Everything we do uses energy.
- Until the energy system is decarbonized, everything we do generates emissions.
- Everyone is conflicted.

Intersection with Cultural Conflict

- Culture wars in the US and Australia:
  - encompass nearly all issues now, but the environment is a particular focus;
- Industrial vs post-industrial world views;
- Deep Green and Dark Brown.

What to Do with Super-Wicked Problems

- Applied forward reasoning (Levin *et al.*, Bernstein *et al.*):
  - projections and possible future rather than predictions;
- Communications:
  - given better understanding;
- Coalitions and constraints (Levin *et al.*, Lazarus):
  - Lock-in commitments to avoid backsliding in the future.

Applied Forward Reasoning

- This is used by IPCC in the scenario analysis.
- This is helpful, but not a panacea.
- Mechanical projections are arguably worse than useless:
  - IEA has consistently underpredicted (or underprojected) renewable energy.

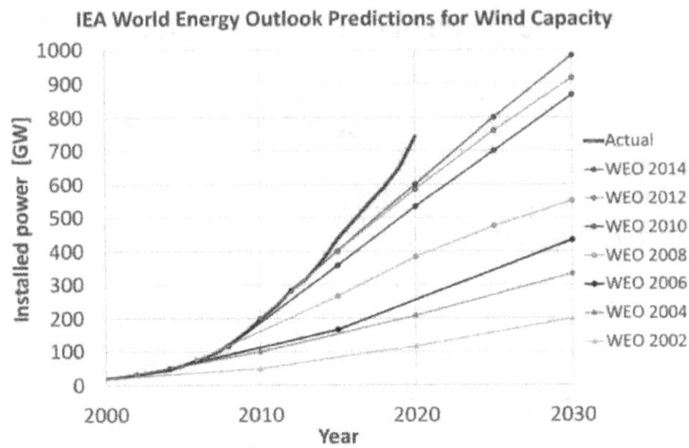

Note: IEA projections of wind power capacity.

Source: https://www.rechargenews.com/wind/stiesdal-net-zero-report-shows-ieas-renewables-forecasts-can-finally-be-taken-seriously/2-1-1016158.

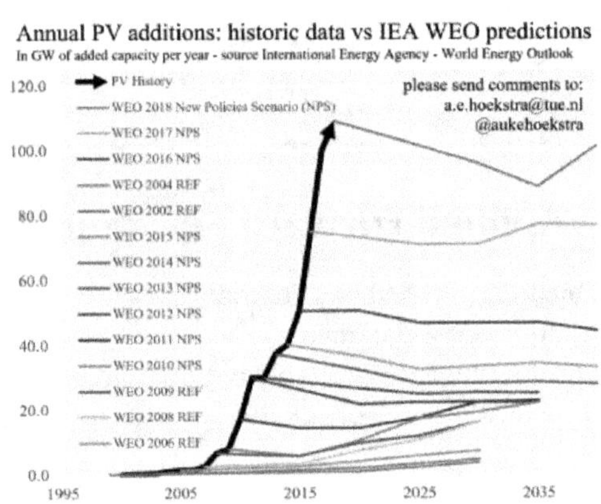

Note: IEA projections of solar power capacity additions.

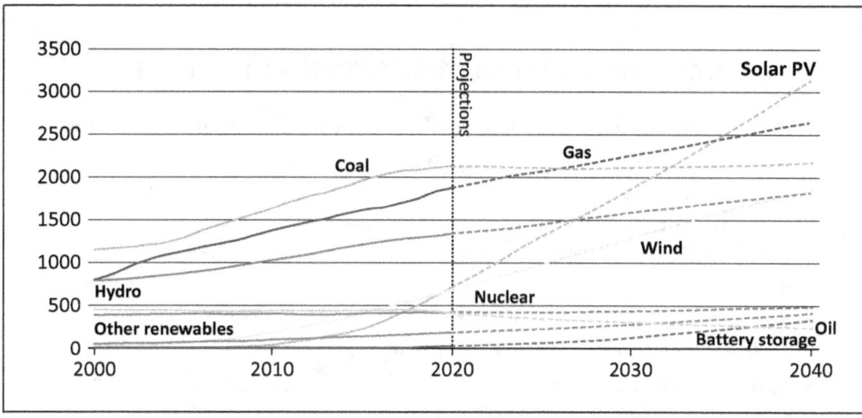

Note: Is this finally getting closer to the mark?

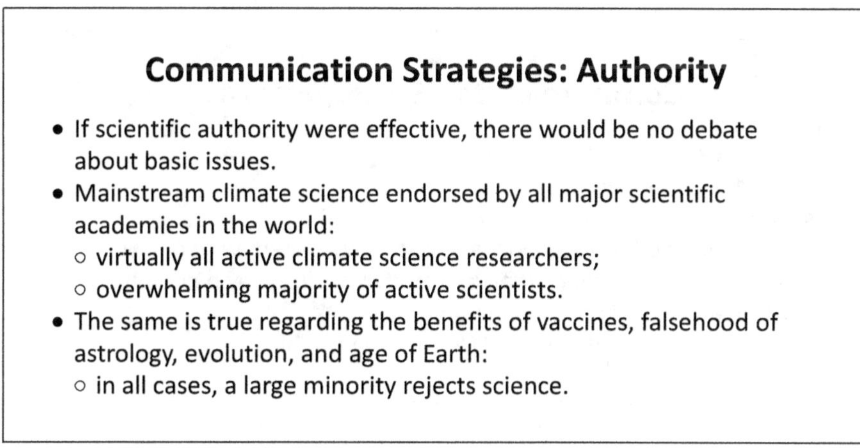

Communication Strategies: Education

- *Idea*: If people were more scientifically literate, they would be more willing to accept the findings of science:
  - This is a hope shared by economists, with even more futility.
- This doesn't work in the face of motivated reasoning.
- Better educated Republicans are more likely to be climate science deniers:
  - https://www.nytimes.com/interactive/2017/11/14/upshot/climate-change-by-education.html.
- Education may be counterproductive to the extent that it improves skills in debate but not in valid reasoning.

Communication Strategies: Facts

- Don't work:
  - at least not well.
- Confirmation bias.
- "Doubling down" in response to data inconsistent with prior beliefs.
- Some limited evidence that repeated exposure may be helpful.
- Wikipedia is a good starting point: https://en.wikipedia.org/wiki/Confirmation_bias.

Communication Strategies: Framing

- See Lakoff's *Don't Think of an Elephant*.
- This book presents ideas in ways that appeal to a potentially resistant audience.
- This may work where positions are not anchored in ideology/personal identity.
- This is not the case for climate change.
- See Bernauer and McGrath's "Simple reframing unlikely to boost public support for climate policy".

Coalitions and Constraints

- Form a (super) majority coalition in favor of action.
- Lock in long-term commitments.
- Override or bypass opposition.
- Though easier said than done, this is the only feasible route:
    - Compare response to anti-vaxxers.

Lecture 9

Reducing Emissions: Markets, Regulation, and Planning

This lecture deals with policy instruments for addressing global heating by reducing greenhouse gas emissions. The starting point of analysis is the duality of prices and quantities: Policymakers can either set a specific emission reduction target (a quantity-based approach) or establish a carbon price (a price-based approach) as the primary policy instrument.

Prices in a market economy serve as signals that both reflect and determine opportunity costs. In a competitive market, equilibrium is reached when the price of a good or service is equal to both the marginal (opportunity) cost of additional production for producers and the marginal benefit of additional consumption for consumers.

Market prices and quantities are interdependent. Understanding the duality between prices and quantities in markets is essential for analyzing economic behavior, resource allocation, and the efficiency of markets in meeting consumer and producer preferences.

The duality between prices and quantities in economics is analogous to the duality between the position and velocity of a particle in quantum physics. The Heisenberg Uncertainty Principle states that there is a fundamental limit to our ability to precisely measure both the position and velocity of a particle simultaneously. This principle highlights the inherent uncertainty and limitations in our ability to measure certain physical properties accurately.

Similarly, government intervention can focus on fixing either the quantity of a good (through quantity controls like quotas) or the price (through price controls like taxes or subsidies), but not both simultaneously.

Implementing a carbon tax provides certainty about the marginal cost of emission reduction. However, it does not guarantee a specific quantity of emission reduction, as this depends on how individuals and businesses respond to the tax.

An emission trading regime offers certainty about the level of emissions through a cap on emission allowances. However, it does not provide certainty about the marginal cost of emissions reduction, as this cost depends on the technology available to firms.

The range of market-based measures to reduce emissions includes the following:

- **Carbon Tax:** A carbon tax imposes a price on carbon emissions. Polluters pay a tax based on the amount of carbon they emit. This encourages emission reductions by making carbon-intensive activities more expensive and providing an economic incentive to reduce emissions.
- **Emission Permits (Cap-and-Trade):** Cap-and-trade systems establish a maximum limit (cap) on total emissions and distribute permits to emitters. These permits can be traded among participants. Firms that reduce emissions below their allotted permits can sell surplus permits, while those exceeding their limit must purchase additional permits. This system creates a market for emission reductions, driving down overall emissions.
- **Hybrid Approaches:** Some policies combine elements of both carbon pricing and quantity-based mechanisms. For example, a carbon tax may have a regulatory backstop that imposes emission limits if certain reduction targets are not met.

Alternatively, governments can adopt measures which are not market based, though their effects will be felt through markets. Through regulation, governments can mandate emission limits for specific industries or sectors. Penalties for non-compliance may be regarded as a special kind of price.

Alternatively, governments may provide incentives or subsidies for the development and use of renewable energy sources to promote cleaner energy production. Investment in research and development (R&D), initially reliant on public subsidies, has produced massive reductions in the cost of clean electricity technologies, including wind power, solar photovoltaics, and, more recently, battery storage. Other technologies, such as carbon capture and storage (CCS) and nuclear power, have been less successful.

Readings

Australian Conservation Foundation (2010) Better Than Growth. https://d3n8a8pro7vhmx.cloudfront.net/auscon/pages/1358/attachments/original/1474590438/ACF_Better_Than_Growth_2010_11.pdf.

Quiggin, J. (2019) *Economics in Two Lessons: Why Markets Work so Well, and Why they can Fail so Badly*. Princeton UP, Princeton, NJ.

Policy Instruments

- Duality of prices and quantities:
  - market-based measures;
  - carbon tax;
- Emissions permits;
- Hybrids;
- Regulation;
- Direct action.

Opportunity Cost and Market Failure

- **Recall Lesson 2:** Market prices don't reflect all the opportunity costs we face as a society.
- Market failure covers instances of Lesson 2 where the divergence arises from the non-existence or poor function of a market for some good or service.

Responses to Market Failure

- Create new markets.
- Use taxes and subsidies to change market prices.
- Regulate market behavior.
- Replace markets with planning.

Markets: Prices and Quantities

- This is a fundamental duality in economics.
- **Lesson 1:** Market prices reflect and determine opportunity costs faced by consumers and producers.
- In competitive equilibrium, price is equal to
  - marginal (opportunity) cost of additional production;
  - marginal benefit of additional consumption.
- Market prices and quantities are jointly determined.

The Case of Carbon Emissions

- In the absence of government action, price of emissions is zero:
  - Quantity is that which maximizes profits/utility of the emitter.
- Lesson 2 applies here: Market prices don't reflect all the opportunity costs we face as a society.
- We can attempt to set price equal to opportunity cost through carbon taxes or set quantity equal to socially optimal level through permits.

Carbon Taxes

- Carbon taxes are set a price on CO_2 emissions:
  - Ideally, this is equal to marginal social cost.
  - Market decisions determine the level of emissions.

Tradeable Emissions Permits

- Tradeable permits determine the allowable quantity:
  - Ideally, this is set by the carbon budget consistent with stabilization.
  - Market for permits determines the price.

Equivalence of Taxes and Permits

- Both imply a price on emissions.
- Optimal tax is equal to marginal external costs.
- Optimal volume of permits is the quantity of emissions where marginal private benefit of emissions equals marginal external costs.
- Equilibrium market price of permits is a marginal private benefit.
- Optimal tax equals emissions price with optimal quantity.
- Both yield the same quantity of emissions.

Equivalence of Price and Quantity Controls

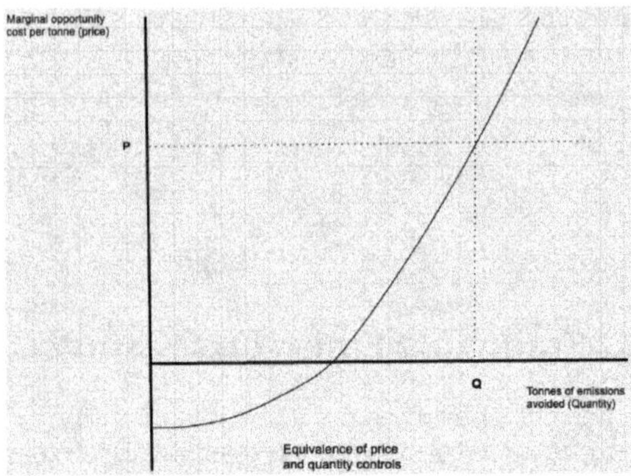

The Uncertainty Principle

- In quantum physics, we can measure the location of a particle or its velocity but not both.
- In an otherwise unconstrained market, we can intervene to fix the quantity or the price, but not both.
- Carbon tax gives us certainty about the marginal cost of emissions reduction, but not about the quantity of emissions.
- The emissions trading regime gives us certainty about the level of emissions but not about the marginal cost.

Uncertainty About Costs

- This is the only relevant source of uncertainty in this case.
- Mitigation requires either
  - increasing the emissions efficiency of what we do (for example, renewable energy) or
  - doing less emissions-intensive things (e.g., using telecommunications instead of travel).
- Both will be costly in general.
- But we don't know in advance how costly.

Who Gains and Loses?

- It's often thought that emissions permits reward polluters, while carbon taxes punish them:
  - This assumes free allocation of permits and no free baseline for carbon taxes.
  - Neither assumption is necessarily true.
- Use of revenue is critical:
  - Good arguments for a revenue-neutral policy returning all proceeds through tax cuts and increased welfare payments.

Example: The EU Emissions Permit Scheme

- This scheme began operation in 2005.
- This covers about 45 percent of EU emissions:
  - electricity, energy-intensive industries, aviation;
  - petrol is heavily taxed in most EU countries.
- Permits were initially given to existing emitters and are now mostly auctioned.
- The volume of permits was designed to reduce over time.
- There is a target of 40 percent reduction on 1990 levels by 2030.
  - increased to 55 percent at the recent summit.

Effort Sharing

- EU has 28 member countries.
- Cap must be allocated among them:
  - National targets are based on Member States' relative GDP per capita.
  - Less wealthy countries have less ambitious targets.
- Such an allocation is achieved more easily in a confederal system like the EU than in a world of separate nation-states.
- Each country must adopt its own policies for sectors outside the scheme.

Hybrids

- Emissions trading with
  - fixed prices (effectively a carbon tax) or
  - upper and lower bounds.
- Sector-specific mandates with tradeable offsets:
  - renewable energy target and certificates in Australia;
  - fuel efficiency requirements in China.

Example: Carbon Pricing Mechanism

- This was introduced by the Gillard government in Australia in 2012:
  - followed the failure to achieve political consensus on the Carbon Pollution Reduction Scheme (CPRS);
  - replacement of Turnbull as opposition leader and Rudd as PM.
- This was initially a fixed price emissions trading scheme, with a plan for variable price later:
  - seen to violate the pre-election promise of "no carbon tax";
  - contributed to the defeat of Gillard as PM;
  - more casualties on this issue: Abbott, Turnbull (again), Morrison (?);
  - a 'wicked problem' indeed.

Example: The Renewable Energy Target

- There was a requirement for electricity retailers to include a given proportion of renewable energy in their output.
- Those with a shortfall can buy Large Generation Certificates (LGC) from those who exceed the required target:
  - certificate price in $/MWh.
- All carbon-based generation was treated equally, regardless of emissions intensity:
  - brown coal 1.3t/MWh, black coal 1t/MWh, HELE a little less, gas 0.5 t/MWh;
  - Clean Energy Target proposed by Finkel would fix this.

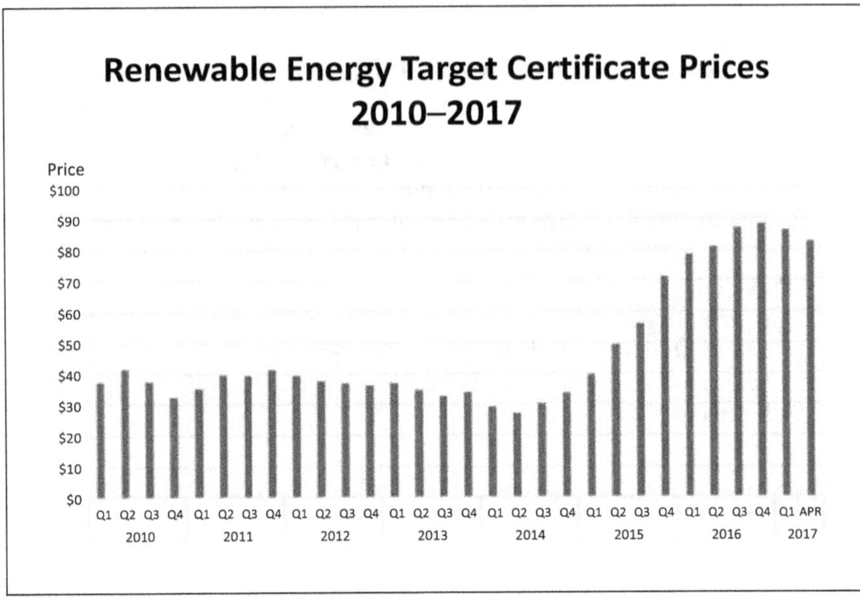

Source: https://www.energycouncil.com.au/analysis/tracking-ret/.

Example: The Emissions Reduction Fund

- This was introduced by the Abbott government after scrapping the Carbon Pricing Mechanism:
  - an auction-based scheme;
  - designed to conceal its reliance on an implicit carbon price;
  - fund nearly exhausted by 2018, to be topped up if LNP re-elected.
- Problems included
  - additionality;
  - insufficient funding;
  - scalability.

Regulation

- Direct controls, with violations punishable by civil or criminal action;
- No explicit role for prices;
- Various forms:
  - prohibition of damaging activities,
  - technology mandates,
  - efficiency and emissions standards;
- Often inefficient, but popular.

When is Regulation Helpful?

- It is helpful in cases where one person makes decision to buy, but another bears the cost of operation:
  - rental properties and solar PV,
  - new and second-hand car buyers.
- It is helpful in bounded rationality and myopia:
  - light bulbs.

Example: Light Bulbs

- Incandescent light bulbs are
  - dominant lighting tech since Edison 1880;
  - cheap but short-lived and energy efficient.
- Regulation set efficiency standards that incandescent light bulbs couldn't meet.
- This was replaced by a series of alternatives, culminating in LEDs:
  - higher initial cost, but lower lifetime cost.
- https://www.nytimes.com/interactive/2019/03/08/climate/light-bulb-efficiency.html.

Example: Vehicle Fuel Efficiency

- The US and other countries introduced corporate average fuel efficiency (CAFÉ) standards in the 1970s, following sharp increases in the price of (imported) oil.
- Now, this is used as a tool to reduce CO_2 emissions.
- The Obama Administration set ambitious targets for 2025.
- This involves a complex formula depending on the mix of small and large vehicles, cars vs SUVs/trucks.

Opposition to Standards

- The Trump Administration rolled back the Obama standards:
  - New standards were imposed under Biden.
- The Australian government has rejected proposals:
  - Even though this meant consumers would save over the lifetime of the car.
  - Oil industry wants to keep using high sulfur fuel.
  - Car dealers put priority on performance over economy.

Example: Electric Vehicles

- Electric vehicles are now cost-competitive with internal combustion engines (ICE).
- European countries have set dates for phasing out sales of new ICEs.
- Emissions reductions depend on the source of electricity.
- On current trends, decarbonization of electricity will be complete well before ICE phase-out.

Planning

- This involves setting and implementing specific goals for the adoption of particular technologies.
- There is no exposure to, or reliance on, market signals.
- This is a blunt instrument, but may be the most effective.

Planning: Partial Planning

- Government action is needed to
  - build renewable electricity generation;
  - close coal-fired power stations;
  - prohibit new coal mines;
  - build infrastructure for electric vehicles.

Comprehensive Planning

- *Energyiewende*:
  - planned transition from nuclear + coal to renewables (+ gas?).
- Green New Deal:
  - combine social reforms, infrastructure energy, transition;
  - the Biden version: American Jobs Plan.
- Australia Technology Roadmap:
  - "stretch goals" for CCS, hydrogen other technologies;
  - planning by wishful thinking?

What To Do Next

- Delays since the 1990s mean that it is too late to insist on "first-best" price-based policies.
- This should still apply benefit–cost analysis with an implicit carbon price.
- Any policy that yields reduced emissions at a sufficiently low cost should be supported.
- US currently applies around $US38/tonne $CO_2 \approx$ $A54/tonne:
  - compare the price implied by the Renewable Energy Target.

Lecture 10

The Outlook for Climate Policy in Australia

This lecture begins with a comparison between the Paris target of constraining heating to 1.5 °C and a 'current policy commitment' projection of 3 degrees. The consequences of 3 degrees of heating were analyzed in a report prepared for the Australian Academy of Science by an expert panel of 14 mostly natural scientists, but including one economist (me).

The report focuses on the consequences of 3 °C of global warming for the following four areas of importance to Australia's future:

- ecosystems,
- food production,
- cities and towns,
- health and well-being.

The consequences for natural ecosystems would be catastrophic:

> *Critical thresholds in many natural systems are likely to be exceeded as global warming of 1.5 °C above pre-industrial levels continues. These impacts will increase as global warming reaches 2 °C and beyond, with iconic ecosystems such as the Great Barrier Reef and the world heritage-listed Kakadu National Park being severely affected.*

Consequences for food production, city life, and health and well-being would be severe, although adaptation would be possible.

The report showed that the success of the Paris Agreement is vital to Australia. Yet, our own progress in reducing emissions has been very limited. The next section of the lecture describes the policy actors whose interaction determines the outcomes of climate policy. These include Commonwealth and state governments, business and environmental groups, and the 'commentariat', including traditional and social media.

Scientists and scientific organizations also play a role. They have made significant contributions to the intellectual understanding of the issues, but have had limited (arguably zero) influence on political outcomes. This outcome is consistent with views of the policy process, which place more weight on organized interests than on technical expertise.

The role of the media and commentariat reflects the general trend toward cultural political polarization over recent decades. Most of the active debate is between denialists (the News Limited group owned by the Murdoch family and talk radio) and activists (the Guardian and Crikey media groups and most social media). Traditional media, such as the Australian Broadcasting Commission, attempt to steer a middle course, generally reporting the scientific consensus, while providing a platform for denialist opinion.

The next section of the lecture is a sector-by-sector analysis of the possible avenues for reducing emissions:

- Electricity
- Transport
- Households
- Industry

The lecture concludes with a discussion of the possible economic benefits to Australia of exporting solar and wind energy, either directly using high-voltage cables or embodied in products such as 'green' hydrogen (produced by electrolytic splitting of water molecules into hydrogen and oxygen, and ammonia).

Readings

Australian Academy of Science (2021) *The Risks to Australia of a 3°C Warmer World.* https://www.science.org.au/supporting-science/science-policy-and-analysis/reports-and-publications/risks-australia-three-degrees-c-warmer-world.

Quiggin, J. (2019) *Economics in Two Lessons: Why Markets Work so Well, and Why they can Fail so Badly*. Princeton UP, Princeton, NJ.

Christoff, P. (2013) *Four Degrees of Global Warming: Australia in a Hot World.* Routledge, London and New York.

Where Are We Heading?

- The three-degree baseline.
- Who are the policy actors?
- What are the policy objectives?
- Sector by sector.
- Policy settings.

Where is the World Heading?

- Commitments when the report was released implied 3 degrees of heating ± 1.5.
- An improvement on 4 degrees seemed likely after limited agreements at Copenhagen COP 2009.
- New commitments at the Biden summit have lowered this by about 0.2 degrees.
- https://climateactiontracker.org/publications/global-update-climate-summit-momentum/.
- Anything above 2 degrees will have disastrous consequences for Australia.

Australia at 3 Degrees

- See report by the Australian Academy of Science.
- The report focuses on the consequences of 3 °C of global heating for four areas of importance to Australia's future:
  - our ecosystems;
  - food production;
  - cities and towns;
  - health and wellbeing.
- Expert panel of 14 included mostly natural scientists +1 economist (me).

Is 1.5 Degrees Impossible?

- Executive summary states "1.5 degrees of warming is virtually impossible to achieve":
  - added after final review;
  - misleading.
- In the IPCC language, "1.5 degrees" is shorthand for "an emissions budget consistent with a 60 percent chance of 1.5 degrees of warming".
- Failure to achieve this budget means the chance of 1.5 degrees warming is less than 60 percent, not zero.

Ecosystems After 3 Degrees of Heating

- Critical thresholds in many natural systems are likely to be exceeded as global heating of 1.5 °C above pre-industrial levels continues. These impacts will increase as global heating reaches 2 °C and beyond, with iconic ecosystems, such as the Great Barrier Reef and the world heritage-listed Kakadu National Park, being severely affected.
- At 3 °C of global heating, many of Australia's ecological systems would be unrecognizable. The decline of Australia's natural resources would accelerate through changing distributions or loss of thousands of species and disrupted ecological processes such as habitat maintenance.

Food Production

- Australian agriculture and food security are already exposed to increased risk from drought, heatwaves, fires, floods, and invasive species.
- Impacts from declining rainfall and more frequent droughts for areas such as south-eastern and south-western Australia would intensify under 2 °C or more of global heating.
- Forestry faces growing pressures from a warming and drying climate: increased fire risks, changes in rainfall patterns, and species-specific pest impact.
- Fisheries and aquaculture industries are impacted by ocean acidification and warming.

Where is the World Heading?

- Close to 90% of Australians live in cities and towns, and will experience climate change impacts from the perspective of an urban environment. The risks of extreme events such as heatwaves, severe storms, major floods, bushfires, and coastal inundation from sea level rise continue to increase and will be more intense and frequent as temperatures exceed 2 °C of heating.

Health and Wellbeing

- More frequent and intense weather events such as heatwaves, droughts, cyclones, bushfires, and floods have direct and indirect impacts on human health, livelihoods, and communities.
- The elderly, young, unwell, and those from lower socio-economic backgrounds are at increased risk.
- Strategies such as improving early warning systems for extreme weather events, assessing the climate resilience of healthcare services, and implementing nature-based solutions (such as increasing green spaces in urban areas) are crucial.

Who are the Policy Actors?

- commonwealth government;
- state governments;
- scientists;
- businesses;
- environmental groups;
- media and commentariat.

Commonwealth Government

- On standard views of the process, the common government should be dominant in setting policy.
- It is not a unitary actor:
  - liberals vs nationals;
  - denialists, lukewarmers, pragmatists;
  - narrow majority in the House of Representatives.
- It has proved incapable of formulating a coherent policy.
- Though it was defending coal until recently, it is now focused mainly on gas.

State Governments

- The state governments are historically subordinate to commonwealth:
  - fiscal imbalance;
  - lack of policy capacity.
- COVID-19 pandemic, electricity market, climate change:
  - policy vacuum at the national level;
  - states have acted independently;
  - generally with voter approval.

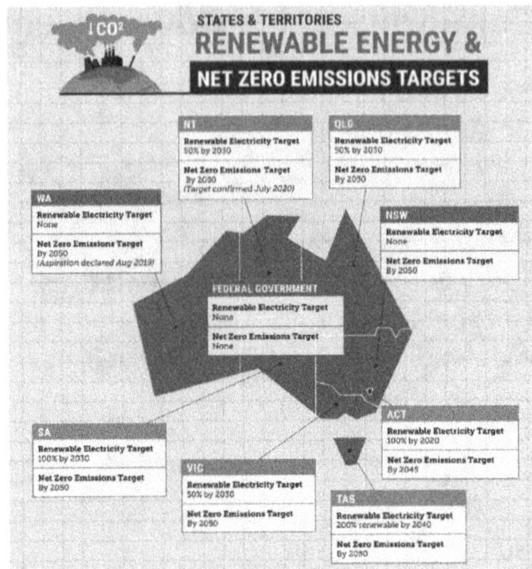

Source: https://www.climatecouncil.org.au/resources/what-does-net-zero-emissions-mean/.

Promoting Zero-Carbon Electricity Generation

- Queensland Cleanco vs publicly owned coal;
- SA already coal-free moving toward 100 percent zero carbon;
- Tasmania: Export hydro and renewables;
- ACT no local generation, wants 100 percent renewables;
- Vic and NSW targets, mixed policies.

Scientists

- Near-unanimity on main conclusions of climate scientists:
  - dissenting scientists, mostly not scientists at all;
  - no true Scotsman?
- Also economists, social scientists, philosophers.
- Statements and reports by academies, associations and individuals.

Businesses

- No unified position.
- Coal and gas industries are opposed to decarbonization.
- Most others, including finance and insurance, want policy certainty and a clear path to net zero.
- But gas seems to have a disproportionate influence:
  - reasons are unclear.

Environmental Groups

- public opinion;
- political campaigning;
- pressure for divestment;
- direct action.

Media and Commentariat

- **Denialist/donothingist**: Murdoch, talk radio, IPA.
- **Actively supporting mitigation**: Guardian, Crikey, Twitter, Australia Institute.
- **Centrist, Insiderist**: ABC, Nine, Grattan.

Sector by Sector

- Electricity
- Transport
- Households
- Industry

Electricity

- National Electricity Market is a wholesale electricity market.
- This was set up in the early 1990s, just after the Rio Earth Summit.
- The design structure takes no account of CO_2 emissions.
- It failed to deliver the promised price reductions.
- This was compromised at the federal level by the Energy Security Board.
- States have taken independent action.

Electricity Generation

- There is a general acceptance that coal-fired power will end:
  - a significant shift since Morrison's lump of coal in 2017.
- The government's view is that gas is a transition fuel.
- The global trends include wind, PV with battery backup.

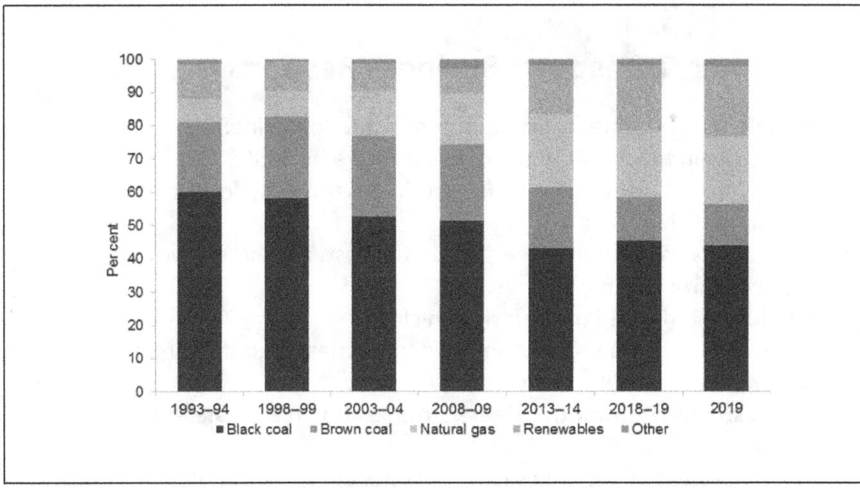

Source: https://www.energy.gov.au/data/electricity-generation.

Transport

- There is a need to improve fuel efficiency in the short term, electrify in the medium term, decarbonize by 2050:
  - feasible for land transport, more difficult for sea, harder again for air.
- There is support from state governments:
  - but undermined by new road user taxes.
- There is no action from Commonwealth:
  - rejected fuel efficiency targets;
  - ignored electric vehicles.

Transport: Business Responses

- Fuel efficiency targets are opposed by the following: electrify in the medium term, decarbonize by 2050:
  - *Refiners*: Current high-sulfur product is too dirty for many fuel-efficient cars.
  - *Dealers*: With more expensive initial cost, consumers won't recognize lifetime savings.
- Industry is divided on electric vehicles:
  - Federal Chamber of Automotive Industries (manufacturers/importers) want a clear transition plan.
  - Australian Automotive Dealers Association (car dealers) is unenthusiastic:
    - Business model relies on after-sales services, but electrics don't need as much.

Households

- enthusiastic take-up of rooftop solar;
- batteries and electric vehicles;
- demand response;
- energy efficiency.

Industry

- Carbon price would be most efficient, but unlikely to happen.
- Case-by-case technological options include the following:
  - **Aluminum:** Electricity-intensive, needs constant supply, the switch will depend on batteries/hydro;
  - **Steel:** Direct reduction of iron using hydrogen (should fit government strategy);
  - **Cement:** Low-carbon alternatives being developed.

Is There an Alternative?

- Australia could rapidly expand solar PV and win.
- It could export electricity via high-voltage direct current to Indonesia and beyond.
- Or it could be embodied in hydrogen produced by electrolysis (green hydrogen) and ammonia (NH_3).
- There are no real obstacles to electrifying road transport.

Lecture 11

The Global Outlook for Climate Policy

The response to global heating involves a vast multitude of actions taken by governments, businesses, and individual households, far too many to cover in any detail. This lecture will deal mainly with what is happening at a global level, through the UN Framework Convention on Climate Change.

We will draw heavily on the work of the International Energy Agency (IEA). In 2021, the IEA published its report "Net Zero by 2050: A Roadmap for the Global Energy Sector", which "sets out a narrow but achievable pathway for the global energy sector to reach net zero emissions by 2050." The rapid pace of change since then has led the IEA to produce a series of updates, and this is likely to continue. So, while the evidence presented in these lectures was up to date at the time, readers should check for more recent updates.

The path to net zero proposed by the IEA is broadly similar in structure to the transition that is already taking place in Australia and elsewhere. Nearly all the technologies required for a transition are currently available. The main problem is that the pace of transition is too slow. As the graph for "Total Energy Supply in the NZE" (see page 149) shows, we should be seeing a peak in coal demand right now, followed by a rapid decline to negligible levels. Similarly, oil and gas use needs to decline, starting in the next few years.

The first, relatively easy step in the transition is decarbonization of electricity supply, with wind power and solar PV replacing coal and gas as the primary sources. Electricity generated by wind and solar has for some time been cheaper than that generated by new coal-fired power nearly everywhere, and is now cheaper than keeping existing coal plants running in many cases. The big change in recent years has been rapid improvement in the technology of battery storage, which has largely resolved the problems of intermittency and variability. The big problem is the reluctance to close down existing coal-fired power stations, which may appear economically viable in the absence of a carbon price.

The next step in the process is electrification of transport and industries such as steel production, which currently rely on carbon-based fuels. Once again, technological progress has provided a pathway, but the stock of existing capital (internal combustion engine vehicles, the factories that produce them, steel mills based on blast furnaces, and so on) is a big obstacle .

This complex picture is reflected in differing responses to the need to stabilize the global climate. Some countries, corporations, and civil society groups are pushing ahead with rapid decarbonization. Others are seeking to extract as much as possible from coal, oil, and gas while it is still possible to do so.

The trend away from carbon-based fuels, and particularly coal, has been accelerated by the divestment movement. The movement puts pressure on financial institutions such as banks, insurance companies, and international development agencies to cease new funding and divest existing holdings in companies that produce and use carbon-based fuels.

Divestment from coal, oil, and gas has significant implications across various sectors of the economy. One of the most immediate consequences is the potential for a higher cost of capital when initiating new projects. Investors and lenders may demand increased returns to compensate for perceived risks associated with fossil fuel investments, which can drive up the financing costs for new ventures in these sectors.

As divestment efforts gain traction, companies and projects in the coal, oil, and gas industries may find themselves facing a shrinking pool of willing lenders and investors. The reduced access to capital can hinder the development and growth of new projects.

Moreover, divestment often involves the loss of public guarantees and financial support from development banks and export credit agencies. These institutions may reconsider their support for fossil fuel-related projects in alignment with global efforts to reduce carbon emissions.

For existing coal, oil, and gas projects, securing refinancing or managing debt obligations may become increasingly challenging. Traditional lenders could become more reluctant to extend or refinance existing loans as divestment accelerates.

Reading

International Energy Agency (2023) Net Zero Roadmap: A Global Pathway to Keep the 1.5°C Goal in Reach. https://www.iea.org/reports/net-zero-roadmap-a-global-pathway-to-keep-the-15-0c-goal-in-reach.

IEA Report is a Good Starting Point

- International Energy Agency was set up after the oil crisis of the early 1970s:
  - main concern to ensure smooth functioning of markets for oil and gas;
  - "promote secure and affordable energy supplies to foster economic growth".
- This agency is now primarily focused on decarbonization:
  - Report: *Net Zero by 2050 – A Roadmap for the Global Energy Sector.*

Main Message

- Net zero by 2050 is feasible, but current policies and commitments are not yet adequate:
  - The global pathway to net-zero emissions by 2050 detailed in this report requires all governments to significantly strengthen and then successfully implement their energy and climate policies.
  - The report outlines the essential conditions for the global energy sector to reach net-zero CO_2 emissions by 2050.

Three Projections

- Current policies imply median heating of 2.7 °C, which is significantly less than previous projections of 3–4 °C.
- Commitments including 2050 net-zero commitments imply median heating of 2.1 °C.
- Pathway to global net zero by 2050 implies median heating of 1.5 °C.

2.5 Key pillars of decarbonisation

Achieving the rapid reduction in CO_2 emissions over the next 30 years in the NZE requires a broad range of policy approaches and technologies (Figure 2.12). The key pillars of decarbonisation of the global energy system are energy efficiency, behavioural changes, electrification, renewables, hydrogen and hydrogen-based fuels, bioenergy and CCUS.

Figure 2.12 ▷ Emissions reductions by mitigation measure in the NZE, 2020-2050

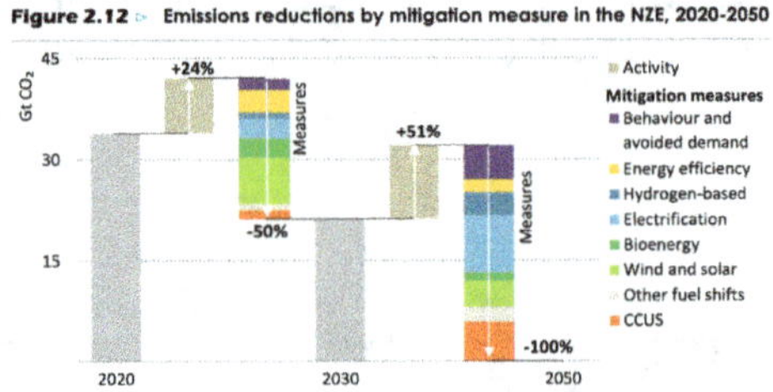

Solar, wind and energy efficiency deliver around half of emissions reductions to 2030 in the NZE, while electrification, CCUS and hydrogen ramp up thereafter

Figure 2.5 ▹ Total energy supply in the NZE

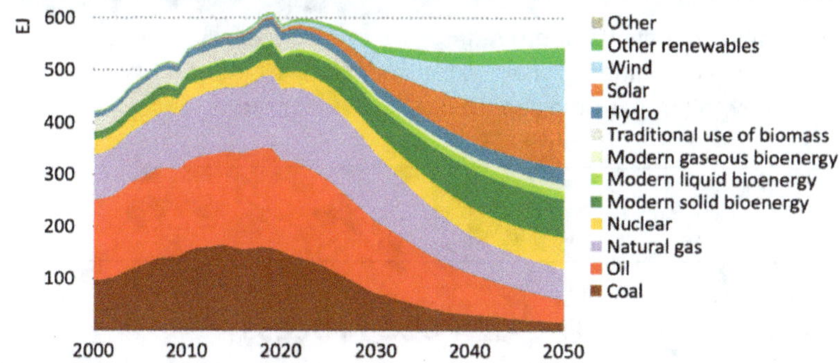

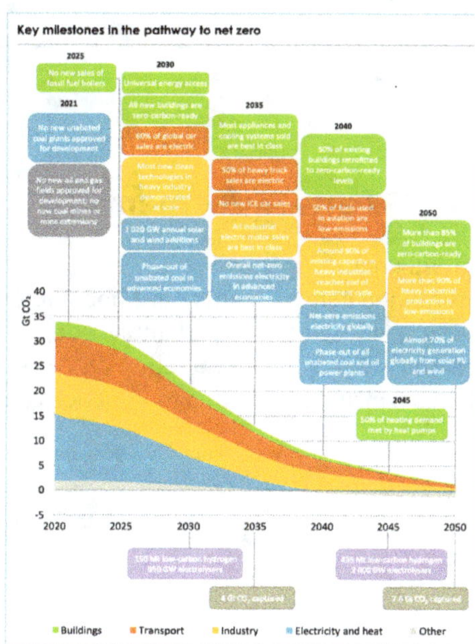

Immediate Requirements

- no new coal plants approved;
- no new coal mines or mine extensions;
- no new oil or gas fields approved for development.

The UNFCCC Process

- UN Framework Convention on Climate Change signed at the Earth Summit 1992;
- Annual Conference of Parties;
- Major conferences every five years;
- Glasgow 2021 being the most recent major conference.

Paris Agreement

- There is an agreed goal.
- Nationally determined commitments have been outlined for 2030.
- Initial NDCs are inadequate and would imply 3 degrees of equilibrium heating, which was expected.
- Ratchet mechanism included the idea to enhance commitment every five years.

From Paris to Glasgow

- Most developed countries have adopted 2050 net-zero goals.
- There is an implied requirement to ratchet up 2030 commitments.
- Movement in this direction was notable at the Biden summit.
- Australia is the most notable exception until now:
  - Outgoing government offered no change to the initial Paris comment of 26–28%.
  - Labor proposed 43%.
  - Greens (and probably teals) support 50%.
  - This may see higher ambition with no change in the formal target.

Net-Zero Commitments

- There could be over 70 countries with net-zero emissions targets, mostly by 2050.
- Many commitments were made in 2020:
  - EU as a whole (with the agreement of all member countries except Poland);
  - Japan, South Korea, China (2060), Canada.
- In the US, Biden adopted the target on inauguration.
- Bhutan and Suriname already had net carbon negative (forestry as the main offset).
- Is 2050 soon enough?
  - We can only get to 1.5 with negative emissions after 2050.

The Ratchet

- There is an increased ambition for 2030 at each Conference of Parties.
- 2050 net zero typically implies a 50 percent reduction on 2000/2005 baseline.
- Many announcements were brought forward to the Biden Earth Day Climate summit in early 2021.
- The COVID-19 pandemic and the Russian invasion of Ukraine have disrupted negotiations.

2030 Commitments at Biden Summit

- US up to 52 percent below 2005;
- Japan 46 percent below 2013;
- Canada 40–45 percent below 2005;
- EU 55 percent below 1990;
- UK 78 percent below 1990 (by 2035);
- Commitments consistent with 2050 net zero;
- Still need more specific policies.

Other Commitments at Biden Summit

- **China:** Peak coal by 2025;
- **South Africa:** Peak emissions by 2025;
- **India:** 450 GW of renewables by 2030;
- **South Korea:** End to global coal finance;
- **Brazil:** 2050 net zero and end to illegal deforestation.

The Holdouts

- These include Australia, Mexico, Russia, Saudi Arabia.
- All but Australia are "problem countries" (as viewed from the US and the EU) in a variety of respects.

Russian Invasion of Ukraine

- Russian supplies of coal, oil, and gas were disrupted.
- This resulted in an increase in world price.
- Other suppliers increased output.
- But, not much investment was noted in new mines, drilling, etc. because long-term prospects were poor.
- Europe was seeking additional supplies of coal, oil, and gas in the short term and accelerated decarbonization in the medium term.

Sub-National Actors

- These included states, provinces and cities.
- Most declared positions are stronger than those of national governments.
- In the Australian and US states, many cities can be included.
- Some states and provinces are going the other way:
  - new coal-fired power in China;
  - coal mine expansion in Alberta, Canada.

Business

- Coal, oil and gas corporations are seeking exit.
- Energy-using corporations pledge to make their own operations carbon-neutral.
- Investors, lenders, and insurers are divesting from coal and (to a lesser extent) oil and gas.

Coal, Oil and Gas Companies

- Most global companies are getting out of coal mining and coal-fired power:
  - BHP, Mitsubishi, Rio Tinto, Samsung;
  - Glencore, Chinese corporations are major exceptions.
- Some oil and gas companies are seeking transition:
  - BP, Shell;
  - Exxon and others sticking with oil.

Energy-Using Companies

- Net-zero promises are becoming the norm outside the heavy industry:
  - a long list https://carbon.ci/insights/companies-with-net-zero-targets/;
  - relying on offsets: airlines, Google (already claims net zero);
  - buying only renewable energy: greenwashing?
  - investing in renewable energy: Apple, Google.

Financial Sector Divestment

- This was initially confined to "ethical investors":
  - "virtue signaling" or "setting an example".
- Now, this is becoming the norm in the financial sector.

Implications of Divestment

- Higher cost of capital for new projects implies the following:
  - limited pool of lenders and investors;
  - loss of public guarantees from development banks and export credit agencies.
- Refinancing difficulty exists for existing projects.
- There is pressure for conglomerates to sell off coal, oil and gas subsidiaries.
- There is also the difficulty of getting insurance.

Effects in Australia

- Coal mining companies are losing access to finance and insurance.
- Adani and Whitehaven are some examples.
- Large energy companies are seeking to divest from coal, oil and gas:
  - pressure to close down operations rather than spinning them off.
- Specialist coal miners are relying on Asian banks:
  - but this is becoming more difficult.
- Regulators issue APRA warning against exposure.

Forces Promoting Divestment

- social license and reputational risk;
- stranded asset concerns;
- liability risk;
- shareholder and employee pressure;
- regulatory risk;
- personal commitment of corporate leaders.

Forces Slowing Divestment

- short-term loss of profitable business;
- existing contracts and business relationships;
- political pressure to support the industry;
- personal commitments of corporate leaders.

The Path of Decarbonization

- Decarbonize electricity.
- Electrify transport.
- Maintain energy efficiency.
- Decarbonize heavy industry.

Electricity: Coal

- Transition from coal-fired electricity well advanced in Europe and North America:
  - easier if there are some existing nuclear and hydro power units.
- Several European countries have ended coal-fired generation.
- Most others have set phase-out dates for 2025 or 2030.
- Germany: Current date 2038, but the recent court case will bring this forward.
- In the US, we have Biden's American Jobs Plan.

Gas

- Methane (CH_4) is a hydrocarbon that is a primary component of natural gas.
- This is a potent greenhouse gas, but combustion produces roughly equal amounts of CO_2 and H_2O.
- Until recently, this was seen as a transition fuel:
  - lower carbon emissions than coal;
  - less local pollution;
  - gas peakers as a backup for variable solar and wind.
- Methane leakage, especially from fracking, is harmful.

Electricity: Gas

- This is now being challenged by the combination of solar and storage.
- Major US and UK corporations are dropping plans for few new gas-fired plants.
- EU is likely to classify gas plants as "unsustainable".
- Gas was central to the LNP government strategy.

Storage

- Any reversible physical process is a potential energy storage technology.
- Batteries: Reversible chemical reactions occur in battery cells.
- Pumped storage is a form of clean energy storage.

Transport

- electric vehicles;
- buses and trains vs planes and cars;
- transport vs communications.

Electrification

- EU aims for 30–40 million vehicles by 2030.
- End of ICE sales is expected by 2035–2040.
- Vehicle manufacturers are announcing similar policies.

China

- China is as important as the entire developed world.
- "A riddle **wrapped in** a mystery inside an **enigma**", described Churchill on Russia.
- China is in a broad geopolitical conflict with the US.
- Policy has fluctuated sharply:
  - spoiler at Copenhagen 2010, positive contribution in Paris 2015;
  - backsliding at Glasgow.

Rapid Growth in Output and Energy Use

- Expansion of wind and solar PV can be noted: 500 GW capacity out of 2500 GW (all electricity sources) installed, adding around 130 GW per year.
- But they are still adding coal, 45 GW in 2022, as provincial governments are still focused on coal.
- There is limited role for gas, hydro, and nuclear power.

Emissions Permit Scheme

- This scheme was introduced in March 2021.
- It had little initial impact.
- Baselines were close to existing emissions.
- There was a low price for exceeding the baseline.
- But this may form the basis for a more effective policy in the future.
- A comparison with the EU would be useful.

International Role

- Chinese banks are still financing coal.
- But there is a big shift toward renewables.
- Belt and Road Initiative is now reaching its end.

Summary

- If the US and China can deliver on stated goals, and other developed countries continue the current trajectory, there is a good chance of meeting Paris goals.
- But there are some big “ifs”.
- Australia remains a laggard.

Lecture 12

Summary and Final Reflections

In the last lecture of the course, I summarize and recapitulate the central issues and offer some final reflections. I begin by restating the central point of Lecture 1, that is, the distinct perspective that a PPE course brings to the analysis of policy problems, integrating political science, ethical and epistemological issues in philosophy, and the economics of resource allocation.

Next, I review the key concepts of the course, as follows:

In Lecture 2, we discuss the science of the greenhouse effect and the history of global heating. A central concept here is that of climate sensitivity, conventionally measured as equilibrium impact of a doubling of greenhouse gas levels relative to pre-industrial levels, that is, from 280 ppm to 560 ppm. Recent estimates are between 2.6 and 3.9 °C.

In Lecture 3, we consider the history of international efforts to limit global heating and the reasons for their limited success.

In Lecture 4, we discuss the central concept of opportunity cost:

- the opportunity cost of anything is what you must give up to get it,
- the social opportunity cost of anything of value is what you and others must give up so that you can have it.

The following are some crucial observations:

Opportunity cost applies to all choices.

Social opportunity cost takes account of all foregone opportunities.

In Lecture 5, we debate the idea of market failure, which arises whenever private and social opportunity costs differ. For global heating, the crucial example is that of externalities. When we burn carbon-based fuels, we do not, individually, bear the costs of the climate damage to which we contribute.

Externalities can be addressed through taxes or the creation of property rights. Economic analysis shows that the two approaches are fundamentally equivalent. Prices and quantities are jointly determined. Fixing the price of emissions through a tax determines the quantity in the market. Conversely, fixing the quantity through an emission trading scheme determines the price. This is analogous to Heisenberg's Uncertainty Principle in quantum physics.

Having developed the idea of opportunity cost, we turned, in Lecture 6 to the emissions equation:

$$C = C/E * E/S * S/G * G.$$

We need to reduce some combination of carbon intensity of energy (C/E), energy efficiency (E/S), energy intensity of output (S/G), and output growth (G).

The opportunity cost of doing less on one of these variables is the need to do more on others. Excessive focus on one parameter may be misleading.

Next, drawing on Lecture 8, comes the concept of 'wicked problems', the central organizing theme of the PPE program at the University of Queensland. As we have seen, the characteristics that make a problem 'wicked', including the lack of an accepted disciplinary authority, the absence of a well-defined solution, and disagreement on fundamental values, are amplified in the case of global heating. The result has been the creation of a new category of 'super-wicked problems' with global heating as the primary example.

Finally, we consider our current position and prospects for the future, drawing on Lectures 10 and 11. Eeyore (the gloomy donkey in *Winnie the Pooh*) and Pollyanna (the cheerful orphan who brightens up the novel and film of the same name) provide contrasting views of the future. Eeyore argues that we should have started major emissions reductions after Kyoto in 1997 and that instead we saw a rapid growth in emissions and a boom in coal-fired power. It is now too late for a quick turnaround in China and India. Furthermore, even if we fix coal-fired electricity, internal combustion engine vehicles will not go away. According to Eeyore's view, the public may accept the need to act on climate change, but most are unwilling to pay the necessary price.

By contrast, Pollyanna believes that unstoppable technical progress in renewable electricity will overwhelm resistance from the coal-fired power lobby. This will lead to cessation of construction and closure of existing coal-fired plants. Further, electric vehicles are now a technically adequate solution for most forms of transport. Similarly, we can reasonably expect innovations to reduce emissions from industry and agriculture.

The lecture ends with my own view of the future. I believe that decarbonization of electricity and most transport will happen before 2050, along with some reduction in industrial and land use emissions. But, this will probably happen too slowly to hold warming to 1.5 degrees.

The result will be substantial environmental damage, such as loss of most existing coral reef systems, along with significant economic damage from sea level rise, heat waves, and wildfires. This will be bad but not TEOTWAKI (the end of the world as we know it).

I finish the course with a 'last chance for questions and comments' and will happily receive the same from readers at the following email address: j.quiggin@uq.edu.au.

Recap of Key Points

Review these slides:

- Lecture 1
  - Nearly 30 Years of Global Efforts
  - Where Are We Now?
  - Wicked Problems
  - Climate Change as a Super-Wicked Problem
- Lecture 2
  - Hansen 1988 Projections vs. Observations
  - Northern Hemisphere Temperatures in Last 1000 Years
- Lecture 4
  - Opportunity Cost
  - Opportunity Cost Applies to All Choices
- Lecture 6
  - The Emissions Equation Explains How Emissions are Determined by a Multi-stage Process
  - All Emissions are Equal

Climate Sensitivity

- This is conventionally measured as the equilibrium impact of a doubling of greenhouse gas levels relative to pre-industrial levels:
  - i.e., from 280 ppm to 560 ppm;
  - For a long time, climate sensitivity was estimated at "between 1.5 and 4.5 °C":
    - improved precision on basic process offset by the inclusion of additional complexities, adding variability.
  - Recent estimates are "between 2.6 and 3.9 °C" (66 percent range).

Market Failure

- This arises whenever private and social opportunity costs differ.
- Free lunches are left on the table.
- Externalities are the most notable in relation to global heating.

Equivalence of Price and Quantity Controls

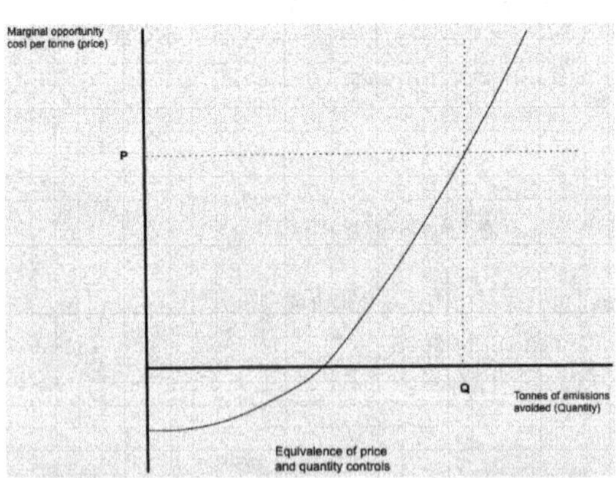

Where are We Going on Global Heating?

- Prediction is always difficult, especially as regards the future (attributed to Niels Bohr, Sam Goldwyn and others).
- Worst-case "business as usual" emissions projections have been averted.
- Learning more about the unforeseen consequences of global heating will be significant.
- We haven't reached catastrophic "tipping points" (as far as we can tell).
- Although there exists an agreement to cut emissions, action so far falls has been short.

View of the Future: Eeyore

- It should have started major emissions reductions after Kyoto in 1997:
  - Instead, rapid growth in emissions and boom in coal-fired power were noted.
  - It is too late for quick turnaround in China and India.
- Denialist and interest group resistance exists in developed countries:
  - US, Australia, Turkey, Poland.
- Even if we fix coal-fired electricity, petrol-driven cars will not go away:
  - gilets jaunes;
  - public may accept the need to act on global heating, but will still be unwilling to pay a price.

View of the Future: Pollyanna

- Unstoppable technical progress in renewable electricity will overwhelm resistance from coal-fired power lobby:
  - lead to cessation of construction and closure of existing plants.
- Electric vehicles are now a technically adequate solution for most forms of transport.
- We can reasonably expect innovations to reduce emissions from industry, agriculture, etc.
- Denialists are an aging minority, even where they now hold political power:
  - Denialist and lukewarmist positions will soon become untenable.

View of the Future: Quiggin

- Decarbonization of electricity and transport will happen before 2050 along with some reduction in industrial and land use emissions.
- But probably this will happen too slowly to hold heating to 1.5 degrees.
- Substantial environmental damage, such as the loss of most existing coral reef systems, could be seen.
- Significant economic damage can be noted from sea level rise, heat waves, etc.
- But it will not be TEOTWAKI (The End Of The World As We Know It).

Last Chance for Questions and Comments

Discuss the issues in class or email me with your thoughts:

j.quiggin@uq.edu.au

Index

www.ingramcontent.com/pod-product-compliance
Lightning Source LLC
LaVergne TN
LVHW022217200926
848481LV00006B/2006
* 9 7 8 9 8 1 1 2 9 0 6 1 9 *